South University Library
Richmond Campus
2151 Old Brick Road
Glen Allen, Va 23060

MAR 1 3 2018

SpringerBriefs in Psychology

Series Editors
Daniel David
Raymond A. DiGiuseppe
Kristene A. Doyle

Epidemiological studies show that the prevalence of mental disorders is extremely high across the globe (World Health Organization, 2011). Moreover, and what is perhaps more concerning is the fact that, despite numerous existing evidence-based treatments for various mental disorders, more than half of those in need of specialized mental health services don't access it and/or do not have access to these treatments (Alonso et al., 2004c; Kohn, Saxena, Levav, & Saraceno, 2004; Wang et al., 2005). Thus, developing and disseminating accessible evidence-based protocols for various clinical conditions are key goals in mental health. This effort would nicely complement the efforts of the American Psychological Association (see Division 12's List of evidence-based treatments), National Institute for Health and Clinical Excellence (see NICE's Guidelines) and Cochrane Reviews (see Cochrane analyses of various clinical protocols) that identified evidence-based treatments for various clinical conditions, based on rigorous literature analyses. However, once identified, one needs a detailed published clinical protocol to deliver those treatments in research, clinical practice, and/or training (see David & Montgomery, 2011). Please submit your proposal to Series Editor Daniel David: daniel.david@ubbcluj.ro.

More information about this series at http://www.springer.com/series/10143

Daniela Eberhardt • Anna-Lena Majkovic

The Future of Leadership – An Explorative Study into Tomorrow's Leadership Challenges

Daniela Eberhardt
City of Zürich, Human Resources
 Management
Zürich, Switzerland

Anna-Lena Majkovic
ZHAW Zürich University of Applied
 Sciences, IAP Institute of Applied
 Sciences
Zürich, Switzerland

Translated and modified from the German language edition: Die Zukunft der Führung – Eine explorative Studie zu den Führungsherausforderungen von morgen by Prof. Dr. Daniela Eberhardt and Dr. Anna-Lena Majkovic. Copyright © Springer Fachmedien Wiesbaden GmbH 2015. Springer Fachmedien Wiesbaden GmbH is part of Springer Science+Business Media.All Rights Reserved.

ISSN 2192-8363   ISSN 2192-8371 (electronic)
SpringerBriefs in Psychology
ISBN 978-3-319-31494-5   ISBN 978-3-319-31495-2 (eBook)
DOI 10.1007/978-3-319-31495-2

Library of Congress Control Number: 2016935195

© Springer International Publishing Switzerland 2016
This work is subject to copyright. All rights are reserved by the Publisher, whether the whole or part of the material is concerned, specifically the rights of translation, reprinting, reuse of illustrations, recitation, broadcasting, reproduction on microfilms or in any other physical way, and transmission or information storage and retrieval, electronic adaptation, computer software, or by similar or dissimilar methodology now known or hereafter developed.
The use of general descriptive names, registered names, trademarks, service marks, etc. in this publication does not imply, even in the absence of a specific statement, that such names are exempt from the relevant protective laws and regulations and therefore free for general use.
The publisher, the authors and the editors are safe to assume that the advice and information in this book are believed to be true and accurate at the date of publication. Neither the publisher nor the authors or the editors give a warranty, express or implied, with respect to the material contained herein or for any errors or omissions that may have been made.

Illustrations: Jana Eberhardt, Copyright © Jana Eberhardt

Printed on acid-free paper

This Springer imprint is published by Springer Nature
The registered company is Springer International Publishing AG Switzerland

The future of leadership depends on connecting people in different ways, in order to expand the collective area of thought and action.
(Daniela Eberhardt)

My Personal Motivation and Thank You

To work with people, to lead them and the fortunes of an organization is versatile, enriching and at times demanding. Almost 30 years ago, at the beginning of my professional life, I was given the opportunity to provide in a team with leadership experts leadership trainings. Very soon my own expertise was enhanced by leadership consulting, applied leadership research, the conceptional design and implementation of management systems and processes and the education of students. In all of those years, I was able to experience in various leadership roles the day-to-day business of leadership and how to lead change processes. As is always the way with intensive experience and research: the more thoroughly you consider a topic, the more questions will arise. The realization of "Think Thank: The Future of Leadership" was a matter close to my heart. The exchange with experienced leadership experts from different industries and disciplines gave me the opportunity to reflect on the issue of "The Future of Leadership" and to gather new insights. The collected findings are summarized in a systematic way and made available to readers.

A warm thank you goes to all people who supported me and us in this work on the future of leadership. To be able to take time out from everyday life and to reflect with thought leaders, professionals and experts on the future of leadership is a privilege. This unique chance was given to me during a sabbatical, which I was able to take as the Director of Institute of Applied Sciences at Zürich University of Applied Sciences during the summer of 2013. I would like to thank Christoph Steinebach, the Director of the Department of Applied Psychology, for making this time out and sabbatical stay in San Francisco and surrounding, and consequently this explorative study on the future of leadership possible.

A special thank you goes to all interview partners, which provided their fascinating perspectives on this topic:

Ajay Bam
Co-founder and CEO at Produk.me, Lecturer in Entrepreneurship and Innovation, Haas School of Business at University of California, Berkeley, Advisor at Padloc LLC

Ed Chaffin
President of IMPACT Group, Founder of the Uncommon Leadership Institute

Gioia Deucher
Leader of the new swissnex office, Brazil

Claus D. Eck
Former Deputy Director Institute of Applied Psychology, Zürich

Laura Erickson
Associate Director, Head of Finance and Operations at swissnex San Francisco

Sabine Erlenwein
Director Goethe-Institute, San Francisco

David Eu
President, InPhenix

Dr. Jeannie Kahwajy
CEO, Effective Interactions

Frederic Mauch
Founder, BioApply

Ken Mooyman
President, Hexagon Geosystems NAFTA

Prof. Dr. Jeffrey Pfeffer
Thomas D. Dee II Professor of Organizational Behavior, Graduate School of Business, Stanford University

T.M. Ravi
Co-founder, The Hive

Dr. Larry Robertson
Associate Dean, Leavey School of Business, Santa Clara University

Dr. Carole Robin
Director, Arbuckle Leadership Fellows Program, Graduate School of Business, Stanford University

Prof. Dr. Chris Sablynski
Associate Professor, Eberhardt School of Business, University of the Pacific

Prof. Dr. Edgar Schein
Society of Sloan Fellows Professor of Management Emeritus

Dr. Cynthia Scott
Consultant, Core Faculty, Sustainable Leadership, Presidio Graduate School

Kate Sherwood
Founder, Execution Strategy, Managing Director

My thank you also goes to the two interview partners which like to remain anonymous. Without all these interviews this work would not have been feasible.

Emina Reissinger from swissnex San Francisco has looked after me during my stay and has recruited a number of different interview partners from the industry, higher education sector and from different disciples. Thank you very much for that!

My thanks especially go to Anna-Lena Majkovic, my co-author, Camillo Steinbeck and Christian Thurn for all their efforts and various commitments in analyzing and writing up the interview and the final report. I cordially would like to thank my daughter Jana Eberhardt for her creative and innovative illustrations of the respective megatrends.

In the final stage of the project, we were actively supported administratively by Yole de Paolo and Bernadette Rufer. Thank you very much!

Zürich Daniela Eberhardt
October 2015

The Future of Leadership: Summary

How will future social, economic and corporate trends affect leaders? What do leaders need to successfully shape the future? What will strengthen leaders in their position? These questions were presented to 20 leadership experts, senior consultants, outstanding academic leadership experts, senior and top managers in an explorative interview study. The interviewees were selected from a part of the world where innovation is business as usual: San Francisco Bay Area and Silicon Valley. On the basis of the following five future megatrends, the study strived to define future leadership developments: Individualization, Transition to Flexibility, Demography, Rapid Social and Economic Changes, Social Responsibility and Sustainability.

The interview analyses include questions which stimulate the reflection about upcoming leadership challenges and future work spaces. Addressed leadership challenges include, for instance, operating in increasingly complex and flexible organizational models and working methods. Further identified leadership challenges in the interviews include working in environments which will be transformed by technological developments and an increasingly diverse workforce, which will require, more than ever, the productive cooperation between generations, sexes and cultures.

The Individualization Megatrend

According to the interviewed experts, the trend individualization suggests that future leaders will have employees who hold highly individualized ideas and wishes and who can act flexibly in different roles. Sometimes employees will work together with colleagues, then with partners, then with business rivals. Workers are aware of their professional abilities and what to expect from modern working settings – and put forward respective demands. Thus, it will become increasingly important to adopt a flexible leadership style in order to build relationships and, more than ever, to balance diverging interests. Or, to quote Carole Robin, who is responsible for leadership training at the MBA program at Stanford University: "Leadership is going to become more and more about being good at influencing others."

The Transition to Flexibility Megatrend

The interviewed experts believe that employees gather their information from various sources, practice extensive networking and hold a number of more or less reliable friendships. For leadership, transition to flexibility describes the provision of orientation in rapidly changing structures. The complexity and amount of data has to be disassembled into useful units. Virtual and face-to-face communications have to be adjusted accordingly. The key aspect will no longer be to provide employees with information, but to provide focus within the complexity of given information and options. Jeffrey Pfeffer, professor of organizational behavior at Stanford University, states: "So it's become a difference in degree rather than kind, but the leaders still need to keep people focused on what they need to be doing, and the people need to keep themselves focused of what they need to be doing."

The Demography Megatrend: The Aspect of Age

For leadership this trend means, in the opinion of experts, to convey important information according to the preferences and strengths of various age groups through online channels (for the "digital natives") and in direct conversations. It is equally important to create awareness for the specific characteristics of different age groups, to allow for positive encounters and forms of cooperation between generations, for example in mixed-age teams. Lifelong learning, knowledge transfer and mutual mentoring between generations represent additional opportunities of bringing different age groups together.

The Demography Megatrend: The Aspect of Gender

For the future of leadership, the interviewed experts recommend adding the topic of gender equality to leaders' agenda. To build a gender-sensitive culture, provide networks and mentor schemes, pay attention to a balanced workforce via human resource strategies and proceed in a gender-neutral manner in talent management. For the trend demography, Ravi, co-founder of The Hive, describes this issue in a nutshell: "If you are not taking the best elements and best resources that are available you are hurting your own ability to run a great organization. You're limiting yourself. And so that is kind of a mistaken notion that homogeneity can kind of help reduce friction and that's good, but that's not really the case if you want a high performing organization."

The Rapid Social and Economic Changes Megatrend

Regarding this trend and future leadership, the experts recommend a promotion of cultural diversity, personal development of one's own way of thinking and expanding one's horizon. It is about connecting people with different cultural backgrounds to build and lead intercultural teams, and to quickly adapt one's personal leadership style in light of rapid economic, national and political changes. Ed Chaffin, founder of Uncommon Leadership Institute, summarizes the issue as follows: "We have become interconnected across cultures, across economies and the leaders, who doesn't understand the different motivations of people from different cultures is not going to survive, and will not be the leaders who develop the next generation of leaders."

The Social Responsibility and Sustainability Megatrend

Leadership experts demand a balance between profit and responsibility in leadership practices, that all employees act as role models and stand up for sustainable practices. It is about dedication to sustainable leadership, a sharpening of one's own perception of sustainable management and the establishment of feedback loops including a communication of managerial consequences. In order to initiate change and awareness processes Ed Schein recommends to proceed top down: "Top-down always is the only way you can begin a cultural change."

Main Conclusions for the Future of Leadership

The leaders of the future will not only need to be more proactive than ever but also have to respond to a variety of short-term requirements. Various technical and social skills such as communication via social media and new forms of transparency, networking, communication and coordination are classified as central leadership skills. Altered environments such as the digital transformation, demographic trends and the global nature of business require, and enable, new forms of cooperation between people with widely varying backgrounds, linked by new forms of communication worldwide. The expectations and opportunities will become more diverse as the pace of action and availability of possible courses of action will continuously increase. Organizations, groups and individuals have not increased their repertoire of actions to the same extent as these diverse claims have evolved: We all hold a certain (limited) repertoire of action that has always assisted us and that we reactivate for the accomplishment of new tasks. It remains questionable, however, whether our long-established behavioral and perception patterns, alongside increasing work pressure and even faster changing work environment, are enough to cope with future challenges.

We do not only witness growing corporate challenges such as rapid innovation cycles, technological development, global orientation of companies and new ways of working. The individual claims of corporate actors are becoming more diverse and more individualized and are increasingly claimed by employees. The implications for leaders relate to the growing complexity in leadership and a challenge to align these individual claims to the needs of the organization. In order to cope with the corresponding intensification of leadership dilemma, resilient leaders are in demand. These leaders know what they stand for, stand up for the concerns of the organization and the people and have access to sufficient personal resources.

Contents

1 **Megatrends as a Challenge for the Future of Leadership** 1
   1.1 Megatrends and the Characteristics of Trend Research 1
   1.2 Trends Related to the Study 3
   1.3 Trend 1: Individualization 3
      1.3.1 Personal Leadership 4
      1.3.2 Co-leadership 5
   1.4 Trend 2: Transition to Flexibility 5
      1.4.1 Liquid Leadership 6
      1.4.2 Complexity Leadership 7
   1.5 Trend 3: Demography 8
      1.5.1 Age-Related Leadership 9
      1.5.2 Gender-Related Leadership 11
   1.6 Trend 4: Rapid Social and Economic Changes 11
      1.6.1 Change Leadership 13
      1.6.2 Intercultural Leadership 14
   1.7 Trend 5: Social Responsibility and Sustainability 15

2 **Study "Think Tank: The Future of Leadership"** 19
   2.1 Descriptive Characteristics of the Interview Partners 20
      2.1.1 Current Professional Role 20
      2.1.2 Prior Education 20
      2.1.3 Career Experience 21
   2.2 Method 21
      2.2.1 Development of the Coding Scheme 22
   2.3 Results 24
      2.3.1 Current Leadership, Career and Work Challenges 24
      2.3.2 What Strengthens Leaders in Their Leadership Roles? 26
   2.4 Trend 1: Individualization 26
      2.4.1 Leadership Style: "Personal Leadership" 28
      2.4.2 Leadership Style: "Co-leadership" 28

2.5		Trend 2: Transition to Flexibility	31
	2.5.1	Leadership Style: "Liquid Leadership"	31
	2.5.2	Leadership Style: "Complexity Leadership"	32
2.6		Trend 3: Demography	34
	2.6.1	Leadership Style: "Age-Related Leadership"	35
	2.6.2	Leadership Style: "Gender-Related Leadership"	36
2.7		Trend 4: Rapid Social and Economic Changes	38
	2.7.1	Leadership Style: "Change Leadership"	38
	2.7.2	Leadership Style: "Intercultural Leadership"	39
2.8		Trend 5: Social Responsibility and Sustainability	39
	2.8.1	Leadership Style: "Sustainable Leadership"	41
2.9		Challenges, Development Opportunities and Important Competencies for Future Leaders: Conclusions	42
2.10		Future Essential Skills for Followers	42

3 Leadership of the Future: Everything Different or Same Old Same Old? 45

3.1	Personal Conclusion	45
3.2	What Remains?	45
3.3	What Does the Future Hold?	46
3.4	Anything New or Same Old Same Old?	49
3.5	Something to Think About: Possible Action Points and Competencies	50
	3.5.1 Individualization	50
	3.5.2 Transition to Flexibility	51
	3.5.3 Demography	52
	3.5.4 Rapid Social and Economic Changes	53
	3.5.5 Social Responsibility and Sustainability	53
3.6	Leadership of the Future	54

Appendix 55
List of Interview Partners 55
Questionnaire 57
    The IAP Institute of Applied Psychology 60

References 63

List of Figures

Fig. 1.1	Summary of trend Individualization	4
Fig. 1.2	Summary of trend Transition to Flexibility	6
Fig. 1.3	Summary of trend Demography	10
Fig. 1.4	Summary of trend Rapid Social and Economic Changes	13
Fig. 1.5	Summary of trend Social Responsibility and Sustainability	16
Fig. 2.1	Current role	20
Fig. 2.2	Career experience	21
Fig. 2.3	Leading positions (industries)	22

List of Tables

Table 2.1	Summary of main categories	23
Table 2.2	Summary of current work and leadership challenges as consultants and HE providers	25
Table 2.3	Summary of personal current work and leadership challenges as a leader/manager	25
Table 2.4	Summary of elements which strengthen the interviewees as consultant/HE providers	26
Table 2.5	Summary of elements which strengthen the interviewees as leaders/managers	27
Table 2.6	Summary of leadership style: "Personal leadership"	29
Table 2.7	Summary of leadership style: "Co-leadership"	30
Table 2.8	Summary of elements which strengthen the interviewees in relation to the trend Individualization	30
Table 2.9	Summary of leadership style: "Liquid leadership"	32
Table 2.10	Summary of leadership style: "Complexity leadership"	33
Table 2.11	Summary of elements which strengthen the interviewees in relation to the trend transition to flexibility	34
Table 2.12	Summary of leadership style: "Age-related leadership"	35
Table 2.13	Summary of leadership style: "Gender-related leadership"	36
Table 2.14	Summary of leadership style: "Change leadership"	38
Table 2.15	Summary of leadership style: "Intercultural leadership"	40
Table 2.16	Summary of elements which strengthen the interviewees in relation to the trend rapid social and economic changes	40
Table 2.17	Summary of leadership style: "Sustainable leadership"	41
Table 2.18	Summary of conclusions drawn: future leadership challenges	43
Table 2.19	Summary of future essential skills for followers	44

Chapter 1
Megatrends as a Challenge for the Future of Leadership

- How is leadership influenced by societal, social and economic trends?
- What impact does this have on the roles and tasks of leaders?
- Which characteristics and skills do leaders need to successfully shape the future?
- What strengthens leaders in their leadership positions and what will help them in the future to successfully manage their leadership role and tasks?

If leadership should be shaped proactively, a consideration of future leadership challenges and an investigation into the relevance of diversity matters in leadership is needed. In order to answer these questions, central megatrends were presented to leadership experts in an explorative interview study. The interview participants were asked for their personal evaluations and assessment of changes in the future of leadership.

The following five megatrends were discussed with regard to their impact on the future of leadership with the interviewed experts:

- Trend 1: Individualization
- Trend 2: Transition to Flexibility
- Trend 3: Demography
- Trend 4: Rapid Social and Economic Changes
- Trend 5: Social Responsibility and Sustainability

1.1 Megatrends and the Characteristics of Trend Research

Trends define major social, economic, political, and technological changes which need substantial times frames to develop. Megatrends exert their influence in various life domains and tend to last for longer time periods (Kotler, Keller, & Bliemel, 2007).

Megatrends are suggested to last for a period of 30–50 years, to be global in their nature and to survive temporary "backlashes" (Horx, Huber, Steinle, & Wenzel, 2009).

In trend research, usually not including the forecast but the realization, observation, analysis and the development of opportunities of trends are the core issue (Horx et al., 2009). Representative examples of megatrends are globalization or urbanization.

Based on megatrends, additional trends such as consumer trends, fashion trends, trends in technology and socio-cultural trends are widely discussed. However, the latter listed trends do not hold equally long lifecycles as megatrends and do not have such lasting impact on society.

A variety of terms and definitions predicting major economic and social trends can be identified that have already gained public interest. Different authors use varying concepts to describe megatrends or varying numbers of potentially occurring megatrends. According to Horx et al. (2009) the following section represents examples of future trends for this decade:

- *Silver society*: A modified aging process characterizes work, culture and leisure in society. The retirement age should be postponed to a later date; the healthy active older people re-define society (e.g., by staying in the workforce, engaging in volunteering etc.)
- *Female shift*: Traditional role models dissolve more and more (in professional and private life). Women are being promoted into leadership positions and men are incorporated more into domesticity, combining work and family life.
- *Education/new learning*: Through digital media a constantly growing learning and knowledge base has become easily accessible for a wider audience. This leads to an excessive supply of information. As a result of this development, new forms of learning (e.g. e-learning) and lifelong learning become increasingly important.
- *Connectivity*: Networking on technical, and to a greater extent social, levels will be of growing relevance. A development towards openness is changing companies and governmental structures. Transparency becomes highly important for society.
- *Globalization*: The boundaries between first, second and third world become blurred by various interconnections of economic collaboration. On the basis of their economic success, emergent countries will demand more political power.
- *Urbanization*: Biospheres become increasingly urban. Cities develop more than ever into the cultural, economic and creative centers of the world.

The above mentioned and similar trends are widely observed and described. For the interviews of the leadership experts a selection of megatrends was made.

1.2 Trends Related to the Study

The current study introduced the following five future megatrends.

- Trend 1: Individualization
- Trend 2: Transition to Flexibility
- Trend 3: Demography
- Trend 4: Rapid Social and Economic Changes
- Trend 5: Social Responsibility and Sustainability

Trends 1–3 were introduced according to Gürtler (2013), who describes these trends and theoretically reflects upon their consequences for leadership. Those trends were expanded with additional trends which are currently widely debated. An identical interview structure with a focus on future trends was used for each individual trend. For each trend, associated leadership styles were presented, proposing respective future leadership developments and considering certain coping mechanisms for handling the challenges of this specific trend. The interview partners were first asked to comment on the expected impact on the suggested leadership styles and on the leaders' role and tasks. In addition, for each future trend the interviewees were required to identify elements which will strengthen the position of leaders and in turn allow them to be successful in their leadership role (in the future).

1.3 Trend 1: Individualization

Individualization as a trend is concerned with individuals who are focused more on themselves than the community. The individual themselves shape their curriculum vitae and incorporate less external influences. Parallel to the development of individuals runs the development of organizations. An ongoing "individualization" can also be observed in organizations.

Individualization focuses on the aims and wishes of the individual more than ever before. People strive for autonomy in their life planning and prioritizing their own decision making instead of being influenced by others. This social and cultural change leads to a growing demand of more flexible work conditions and different claims at work (Enste, Eyerund, & Knelson, 2013). According to research of the Hay Group (2011), the Individualization trend can be defined as the growing freedom of choice and the fact that careers play an increasingly important role in the quest for self-fulfillment and self-expression. However, given an observed increase in convergence between private and working lives, individuals are eager to combine personal and professional goals (Hay Group, 2011).

Heterogeneous examples of lifestyles, multiple biographies and varied life structures such as patchwork families or single households are all characteristics of the

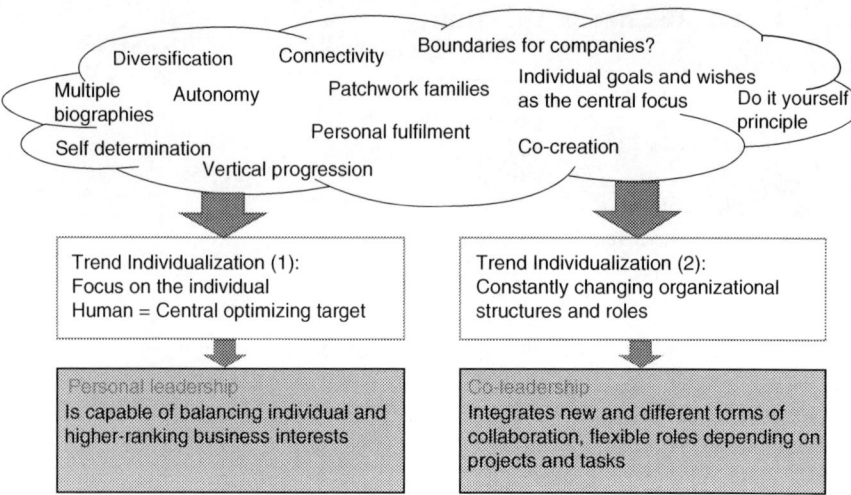

Fig. 1.1 Summary of trend Individualization

Individualization trend and are widely debated topics in both public and scientific literature. An ongoing search for work-life balance is another indicator for an increasingly individualized society (Fig. 1.1).

1.3.1 Personal Leadership

In this study the Individualization trend is divided into two different facets. The first facet includes the current change from process and strategy orientation to human capital. According to Gürtler (2013) one should acknowledge that companies should focus on people rather than processes and strategies, the latter of which can be copied. Therefore, it will become more relevant for leaders to focus on the needs, expectations and aims of individuals. This "new" leadership style is defined as "**personal leadership**". It strives to combine organizational and individual needs at the same time and aims to promote the individual pursuit of success for talented employees (Gürtler, 2013).

The second aspect of the Individualization trend depicts the development that organizational structures and roles will develop flexibly and complement one another. The role within and outside a company cannot be clearly defined anymore. As Peter Waser, former CEO Microsoft Switzerland highlighted in 2010: "*Nobody knows where our company actually ends*".

1.3.2 Co-leadership

As a consequence a new economic logic will emerge. Private and professional networks will increasingly overlap in the future. In order to stay successful in the future, leaders should use the "**co-leadership**" leading style (Gürtler, 2013). Workers fulfill different roles (e.g. project manager, team leader, team member, division manager) as demanded by their projects or tasks, and they require certain skills to remain flexible in their roles. This new form of collaboration crosses corporate boundaries: On one project you may work together with another organization as a cooperation partner, while in the next project this same organization is your competitor. The increasing dissolution of organizational borders and the overlapping of different private and organizational networks have massive effects on cooperation and leadership:

- If employees' networks are integrated into the organization's network (e.g. via LinkedIn or Xing), supply chain management and boundaries of the system "organization" become fluent and less transparent. Who receives information from whom; how does informal decision making take place? All these processes are at least by trend becoming less transparent and more flexible than in those former hierarchically structured organizations structured alongside explicit communication channels.
- When employees' professional networks and organizational boundaries are blurred, work and private spheres become interwoven. Not all activities which are carried out at work are work related and not all activities which are carried out at home count as time off. This new form of cooperation, also described as "dissolution" of work, refers to the liquidation of traditional, spatial, temporal and organizational confines of work. In this respect, the boundaries between work and private life become blurred, to the point where both areas influence each other more and more (c.f. Gottschall & Voß, 2005; Voß, 1998).
- New innovative management concepts are developing, where cooperation and interaction are part of the solution for leading the future.

1.4 Trend 2: Transition to Flexibility

The industrial society is changing into a knowledge-driven society. Service, information technology and a creative workforce are becoming more and more relevant for future business performance. Although work-life balance is crucial for a lot of people, technological advancements will continue to blur the boundaries between private and working lives (Hay Group, 2011).

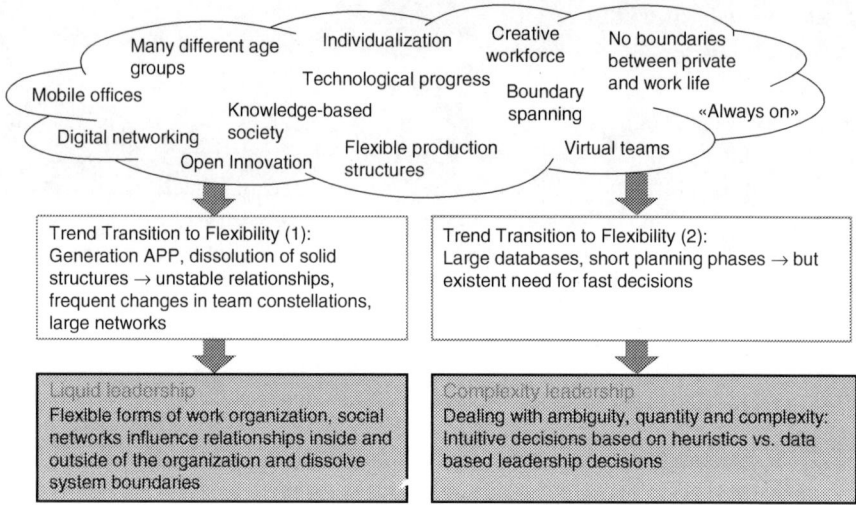

Fig. 1.2 Summary of trend Transition to Flexibility

Technology and the web will both provide the infrastructure and drive the change (Petrie, 2011). Virtual teamwork will rise and extend the complexity of leadership (e.g., Enste et al. 2013). Another key phrase for the Transition to Flexibility trend is "always on", as a synonym regarding increase Internet usage and different smart phone applications (c.f. Yip, Ernst, & Campell, 2011).

Another impact of technological development (for example through the "Internet of Things") is the continuous generation of data by a variety of applications. Theoretically, leaders can, and should, base their decisions on large quantities of data in various fields. The availability of "big data" is one of the major topics of the Transition to Flexibility trend (Fig. 1.2).

1.4.1 Liquid Leadership

In this study the Transition to Flexibility trend is represented by two different aspects. The first aspect refers to an ongoing maceration of solid structures (Gürtler, 2013). Transition to Flexibility leads to unstable relations, frequently changing teams and large networks. Flexible working structures and the integration of social networks are a good way to handle this trend. The corresponding suggested leadership style to deal successfully with associated challenges has been termed "**liquid leadership**".

According to Gürtler (2013) the term "Generation App" (Marxer, 2010) could be used as an idea for the self-organization of social networks. "Likes" and other virtual feedback systems quote the relations and deliver a kind of "company-based Facebook". Flexible workers hold an extensive network which is independent from

1.4 Trend 2: Transition to Flexibility

the hierarchical embedding within the organization, with people inside and outside of the organization. Relations are increasingly characterized by instability; the amount of friends affiliated with "likes" is larger and more heterogeneous than in the former corporate reality. Scoring methods enable the quantification of relations and the delivery of information for building task-related teams. The weak relations of a liquid world highlight a need for strong and reliable relations; technical "matching" of team members cannot overtake a person's responsibility to give orientation. Contrary to this, especially in leadership, the role shifts from "giving information" to "giving orientation and security". Other key phrases describing the future trend of "liquid leadership" are "virtual" teamwork, being part of different private and public communities, and "teaming".

Attributes of "liquid modern times" (Bauman, 2007) are the maceration of solid structures in public and private institutions. In public debates the decreasing participation rate of voluntary work in communities is widely discussed. Based on the relevant project demands the work roles will change. People and organizations have to deal with this liquid situation caused by technical progress and individualization. Based on the idea of liquid democracy (Reichert, 2012) as a system for new participation and decision making processes, Gürtler (2013) suggests "**liquid leadership**" as a solution to these flexible conditions. Each individual becomes part of the process and is encouraged to integrate their competence, or interest, in the process.

1.4.2 Complexity Leadership

The second aspect of the Transition to Flexibility trend is that in a growing complex economic, political and social structure leaders are increasingly confronted with complex business environments. Leaders need to acknowledge that not only have external factors of organizations have become more complex but that processes and factors within their organization have also become increasingly entangled (Döring-Seipel & Lantermann, 2012). Leaders face the challenge of making and implementing their decisions in a highly complex, global and rapidly changing business setting. The term "**complexity leadership**" is proposed to describe the leadership style required to handle the future trend of complexity. This term proposes various ways of dealing with complexity: Traditional views of the decision making-processes are "the better the information, the better the decision". Through enterprise resource planning (ERP) systems, which enable standard data management, Business Intelligence (procedures and processes for systematic data analysis), Intelligent Business Operation (IBO; where data will be processed without intermediate storage in real-time), cloud services (enabling the execution of programs and data storage on external computing centers) and Internet of Things (IoT; connecting physical objects with virtual applications) etc. organizations get more, but also more complex information for their decision making processes. By building on elaborate data analyses, decisions can be made. Via "big data" concepts, technologies and methods will be available which can analyze large amount of information and provide the necessary elements for decision taking. In processing big data, increasing demands and potential problems occur in dealing with: the volume, variance and speed of data (see Feld, Jost & Scheer, 2014). Technical solutions are needed to handle big data (e.g., FuturICT/Dirk Hebling; super computer at ETH university of Zürich or IBM's Watson Computer which is able to build on technologies like machine learning, complex algorithms and natural language processing) which are then delivered to enterprises, institutions and individuals via cloud through cognitive computing.

However, techniques of dealing with "big data" are not guaranteed to secure decision making processes. The increasing availability of knowledge leads to growing levels of uncertainty in identifying definite knowledge. Managers need to deal with the fact that the "unknown" is growing and that they have to develop a sense of how to use this available data. To remain capable of acting alternative forms of decision making are requested (see, Gürtler, 2013):

- "Low information rationality" looks for simple heuristics, rules of thumb or gut decision.
- Deliberately leaving out information and thus improving decision making quality (Gigerenzer, 2008).
- "Start. Try. Fail. Restart. Retry" as a legitimate new business strategy.
- Management concepts with "playful elements" used to be accepted only in creative "niches" but will be useful for different industry sectors and business forms. New innovative projects and start-ups can enter markets more easily than in the past – new ideas have a greater chance of success or failure. The concept of "simply try" will lead to a fast change in branches and enterprises and can be implemented as an "add-up" strategy for established enterprises.

1.5 Trend 3: Demography

The Demography trend will be considered from two different angles: Age and Gender. Apart from those two broader leadership trends, different smaller trends such as diversity, down aging, female power, equality, ageless consuming or value change also have a big impact on demography (Horx et al., 2009).

Since 1990, life expectancy at birth has increased in the majority of countries worldwide by 6 years (WHO, 2014). Humans are not just getting older; they are ageing in a different way. Part of that so called "down aging" is an ongoing change in age related roles e.g. today's 60-year-olds appear like the 50-year-olds of 15–20 years ago. We are aging but tend to stay "younger" in this process. The elderly continue to participate as active members of society (e.g. through working, studying or volunteering). This so-called "silver society" thus changes the traditional rules of retirement (Horx et al., 2009). A continuous "ageing" of our societies will substan-

1.5 Trend 3: Demography

tially change the composition of the future workforce: Cross-generational team work and a rapidly ageing workforce will characterize modern working spaces.

Due to a lack of sufficiently qualified workers people will need to work longer in order to fulfill the needs of the whole society (Enste et al., 2013). As a consequence, participation in the labor market will become more fluent concerning retirement age and people will have to work longer until retirement. In the past, people did not work longer than the official retirement age (on average 65 years in Europe). However, a variation in engagement rate 10 years before official retirement for European figures can be stated. In Italy, approximately 40 % of the workforce is still employed 10 years before official retirement age, while in Germany this is over 60 % and in Switzerland 70 % (Eurostat, 2013).

The "**gender-related leadership**" trend is based on sustained development regarding the equality between men and women. Based on the increasing dissolution of traditional gender roles, far-reaching developments for women and men in professional and social environments can be observed. Albeit still on a small scale some successful, top international companies such as General Motors and IBM are headed by women. Or country responsibilities, for instance at Microsoft Switzerland, or leading management position such as at German Lufthansa and Allianz Insurance are performed by women. Women aspire to leadership positions and men increasingly claim their right to spend time with their families (Horx et al., 2009). Despite corresponding equality efforts of many companies, women are still underrepresented in top management positions. Despite the current development rate where the proportion of women in top positions is steadily increasing, in 10 years women will still take less than 20 % of seats in Europe's governing bodies (McKinsey & Company, 2012).

Governmental support such as tax breaks or increased childcare options and initiatives helping women to reach top management positions are certainly among the basic prerequisites for an increased integration of women into the labor market. However, organizations continue to play a central role in supporting women in their career ambitions.

The postulated Demography trend has a focus on age, termed "age related leadership" and gender, termed "gender-related leadership" (Fig. 1.3).

1.5.1 Age-Related Leadership

Leading multi-generations, using the strength of all ages and taking advantage of different generational skill sets at work leads to a multi-generational approach. To enable knowledge exchange between generations, organizations should combine the experience of older co-workers with the input of ideas and habits from the younger generation. The demographic change thus demands that leaders deal with different expectations, experiences and skills from co-workers of different age-groups. Leaders are faced with the challenge of staying innovative and keeping

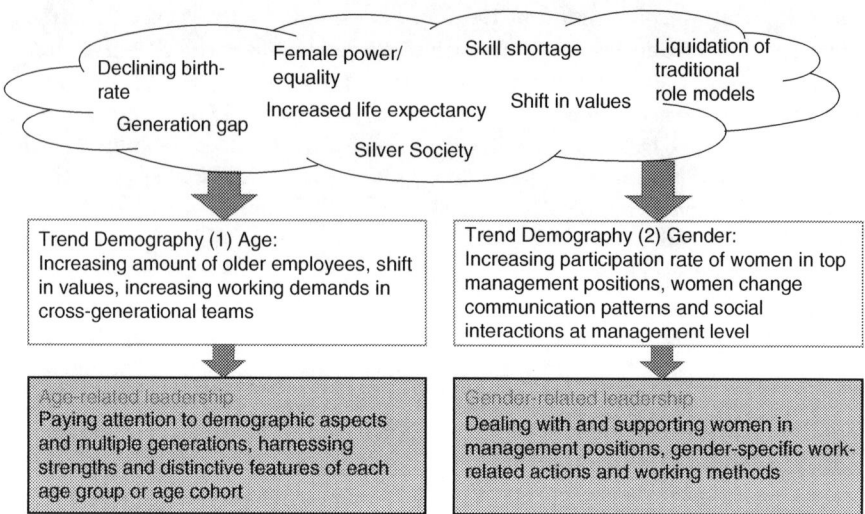

Fig. 1.3 Summary of trend Demography

older co-workers successful and up-to-date, given rapid economic and technological developments.

The proposed leadership style for the future Demography trend refers to "**age related leadership**" and represents a form of leadership which makes the most of a diverse aged workforce. An appropriately targeted "age-related leadership" is known as the only highly significant factor which can enhance the work ability of employees aged between 51 and 62 (Tuomi, Ilmarinen, Martikainen, Aalto, & Klockars, 1997). "Age-related leadership" describes a non-stereotypical attitude towards older workers and the willingness to individually adapt one's leadership style according to the age of employees (Eberhardt & Meyer, 2011; Ilmarinen & Tempel, 2002). "Age-related leadership" can be characterized as communicative, flexible and willing to adapt to age-specific needs of employees for better success.

Attitudes and behavior of leaders with regard to age, or cohort-specific needs and demands (e.g., Babyboomer, Generation X or Millennials), are crucial for using and combining the advantages of each age cohort. For instance when considering individualized personal development plans, individual information processing styles and training issues (Braedel-Kühner, Eberhardt, & Meyer, 2011; Eberhardt, Braedel-Kühner, & Rauch, 2013; Eberhardt, 2013a, 2013b). "Age-related leadership" further integrates age specific competencies and values in mixed-age groups in order to use the diversity and strength of all age groups and improve business across different age groups. In addition to "age-related leadership", the topic of leading a muti-generational workforce is of equal importance. In generation management, the age-specific perspective (i.e. taking into account age in leadership practices and managerial systems) is combined with flexible age-appropriate adaptation of one's own leadership style and promotion of intergenerational cooperation (see Eberhardt, 2015).

1.5.2 *Gender-Related Leadership*

Leaders of the future recognize that organizations which promote a gender balanced workforce and strategically align their diversity management goals provide the basis for sustainable and profitable businesses. Companies with an explicit gender-managing diversity approach will have the potential to serve a broad range of customers and are becoming attractive employers. Moreover, successful companies with a balanced sex ratio at supervisory level have been shown an increased probability of appointing a female CEO (see Cook & Glass, 2014).

Another facet of the "gender-related leadership" trend refers to the notion of potential differences in female and male leadership. The concept of "female leadership" has been extensively researched and widely debated (Eagly & Carli, 2007; Eagly & Karau, 2002). Female leaders climbing the career ladder are expected to take charge and to demonstrate certain leadership characteristics as their male counterparts do while simultaneously highlighting the female "softer" side of leadership. Women thus need to negotiate the feminine and masculine leadership aspects in their leadership approach (Eagly & Chin, 2010). Research has demonstrated that women have a more democratic and participative leadership style than men (Eagly, Johannesen-Schmidt, & van Engen, 2003; van Engen & Willemsen, 2004).

1.6 Trend 4: Rapid Social and Economic Changes

The nature of the global business environment guarantees that no matter how hard we work to create a stable and healthy organization, our organization will continue to experience dramatic changes far beyond our control. (Margaret Weatley, 2003)

The future of leadership is likely to face a number of uncertainties given local and global social and economic changes. With international trade, foreign investments and financial transfers the globalization of the economy has long been in place. The production chain of many goods involves international manufacturing processes and the majority of production sites are internationally located. Advances in communication and transportation enabled and increased the mobility of goods and services. The following developments are additional indicators of this increasing international interconnectivity.

Former emergent countries have become economic giants and claim their right to determine influence on the global community. While the demographic change has led to reduced rates of productive labor force in industrialized countries, the developing countries are facing a surplus of young job applicants.

For the first time in history more people are living in cities than in the countryside. The rise of the knowledge based society leads to an ongoing compression of urban areas and gives them a new relevance as hubs of wisdom. Cities are becoming more than ever cultural, economic and creative centers of the world.

Alongside this development mobility becomes very important in a globalizing world. It has become a prerequisite to our life and our way of doing business. Being mobile is a key factor in getting a desirable job in the future. By discussing the shortage of raw material and a rising demand in sustainability our perception of mobility and our mobility behavior is changing (Horx et al., 2009).

Political and economic crises are an additional factor affecting future leadership decisions. A number of European countries are facing drastic social and economic turbulence. The European Economic crisis has left some European countries in rather unstable economic and social circumstances, threatening long-lasting prosperity and democratic principles of some countries. However, social and political unrests are not limited to the European Union, and are becoming an increasingly global phenomenon (e.g., global threats of terrorism, ongoing turbulence in the Middle East, the Russia-Ukraine conflict, the Syrian civil war).

The above examples highlight that the future of leadership will not be able to rely on solid growth of economic, social and political structures but will need to factor in instability and growing uncertainty. Leaders are likely to face the challenge of how to manage uncertainty and how to effectively adapt organizational structures and business strategies in view of often unprecedented global changes. The situation describes the tense atmosphere in which companies find themselves today. On one hand companies depend on stability and continuity, while on the other hand they are confronted with permanent pressure for change, which requires high degrees of willingness to learn (cf. Classen, 2008). Frequently organizations are not only forced to achieve the same outcomes with fewer resources but to also to flexibly adapt their corporate strategy given rapid changes (see Seufert, 2010).

One visible approach to tackle uncertainty and to make the unpredictable manageable has been to formalize businesses by implementing the 'Institution of Management' (Elbe, 2012). In this regard interactive leadership has been increasingly replaced by steering mechanisms such as Business Reengineering, Quality management or Balanced Scorecard. The apparent advantages of the rationalization of institutions demonstrating possible courses of actions and reducing complexity however also come with associated drawbacks. How should leaders react if situations occur for which no predefined rules or process instructions are suitable? What if flexibility has not been included in detailed and elaborate management systems? In fact, Elbe (2012) claims that the "over-managed but under-led" management steering systems risk shutting out alternative solutions and thus innovative behavior. Instead he suggests that leaders should be strengthened again to act as leaders in providing a vision for the future and to act flexibly by providing resources to tackle prolonged periods of uncertainty and complex change processes. Leaders should work to build resilient organizations, which can overcome crisis and profound changes. Resilient organizations are characterized by optimism and acceptance, are solution-orientated, network-oriented and add to existing management models (Fig. 1.4).

1.6 Trend 4: Rapid Social and Economic Changes

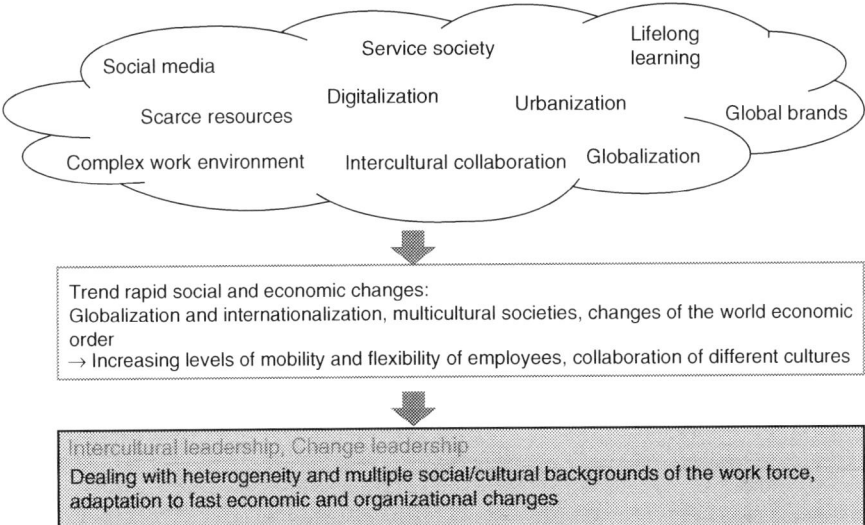

Fig. 1.4 Summary of trend Rapid Social and Economic Changes

1.6.1 Change Leadership

The corresponding leadership style for the trend Rapid Social and Economic Changes has been termed "**change leadership**". "Change leadership" focuses on globalization, internationalization and rapid economic, political and social changes challenging leaders to deal effectively with prolonged periods of uncertainty and instability.

"Change leadership" proposes that the future of leadership does not lie in the provision of routine and predefined managerial processes but in the provision of extra resources enabling organizations to respond flexibly to sudden economic, political or social changes affecting their businesses. "Change leadership" ensures that leaders combine the perspective of the organization and employees and leads through learning processes towards a learning and changing organization (Eberhardt, 2012): "*Leading change implies for me taking responsibility for the process, the results and the people. And this despite things not always running smoothly!*". (Eberhardt, 2012, p. 12)

One leadership style which has been suggested to go beyond a pure rational exchange process between leaders and followers and to be of particular relevance in managing uncertainty and change is transformational leadership (Bass, 1985). As conceptualized by Avolio and Bass (2004), transformational leaders act as role models, providing inspirational motivation, intellectual stimulation and show individualized consideration. Leaders following a transformational leadership style are argued to foster collective team optimism, efficacy and identification with the team's goals (Bass & Riggio, 2006). Transformational leaders are thus argued to activate extra motivational and cognitive resources of their employees which are needed to handle challenging change situations.

1.6.2 Intercultural Leadership

The second facet of the future Rapid Social and Economic Changes trend discusses intercultural forms of leadership. As business push forward into global enterprise, companies are facing mergers and acquisitions on international levels and as higher education systems are continuously becoming more international, intercultural encounters on organization levels will become more likely. Companies thus need leaders who understand and appropriately respond to their business partners' cultural values, practices and norms.

When considering research and the practice of leadership in the context of different cultures, two perspectives were dominant in the last two decades: The investigation of leadership styles cross-culturally, assuming that leaders differ in their leadership preferences as a result of their national and cultural background. The second perspective highlights intercultural encounters and investigates how to optimize associated benefits and minimize possible disadvantages. One representative example of a cross-cultural investigation of leadership styles is the The GLOBE study (Global Leadership and Organizational Behavior Effectiveness Project). The study was conceived in 1991 by R. House (for a comprehensive illustration of the study refer to House, Hanges, Javidan, Dorfman, and Gupta 2004) and included a total of 17,000 leaders from 62 countries worldwide. The goal of the GLOBE study was to describe characteristics and behavioral traits of leaders considered to be good leaders and to describe the existing prevailing values and practices in their countries. On the basis of previously published dimensions, such as Hofstede (1980), and concepts such as power distance (the degree to which one accepts power to be distributed unequally) or performance orientation (the degree to which individual performance and improvement will be rewarded), cross-cultural differences and similarities were reported. Performance orientation was rated as being desirable for all cultural clusters and power distance, even though being witnessed in many countries, was rated as undesirable. With regard to desirable leadership traits, all cultural clusters preferred a charismatic, team orientated and participative leadership style. The latest GLOBE study of CEO leadership behavior and effectiveness gives us detailed insights for example into the extent of which the CEO enacts the behavior of superiors and inferiors. Mission critical are visionary, performance oriented, decisive, inspirational, administratively competent as well as to have integrity. Other behaviors are important as well (e.g., self-sacrificial, collaborative team-orientation, participative) (House, Dorfmann, Javidan, Hanges, & Sully de Luque, 2014).

Relevant in both research and in practice is the question of which leadership competencies are essential to effectively deal with an increasingly diverse workforce and work environment. Research so far suggests transformational leadership styles turn organizational diversity into a positive asset such as team performance or Organizational Citizenship Behavior (Kearney & Gebert, 2009; Muchiri & Ayoko, 2013). Additionally, a strong focus has been put on concepts which incorporate a comprehensive intercultural understanding and global management competencies.

'Intercultural competence' or 'cultural intelligence' are widely debated and immensely variably defined constructs describing various leadership skills. Bird, Mendenhall, Stevens, and Oddou (2010) define the three major elements captured by the majority of intercultural competence definitions: Perception management describing the avoidance of rapid prejudgments and categorization of experiences, relationship management depicting an interest in contacts and sensitivity towards self-development and self-management including optimism, self-confidence, resilience and increased levels of flexibility in private and professional spheres.

In sum, the proposed future leadership style "change leadership" proposes leadership challenges in respect to globalization, internationalization and rapid economic, political and social changes. "Intercultural leadership" discusses leadership challenges being associated with an increasingly diverse workforce due to unification of the economic world order and growing interconnectivity among economies.

1.7 Trend 5: Social Responsibility and Sustainability

As the availability of strategic resources such as raw materials, water, metals and fossil fuels decrease this fuels the potential for global and regional conflicts. Current production processes and consumption behaviors of industrialized countries are leaving their carbon footprint. Companies are increasingly given a larger social and environmental responsibility, which are highlighted in concepts such as Corporate Social Responsibility, Corporate Governance, and Sustainable Development etc. As the investment in clean energy increases, organizations need to work more collaboratively on environmental problems. This includes future challenges of dealing with increasing raw material costs and developing more sustainable environmental friendly processes (see Hay Group, 2011).

Since the financial crisis of 2007–2009, political actors and social authorities in industrial countries have more thoroughly highlighted the significance of social and economic responsibilities of companies. The financial crisis negatively impacted employment, home ownership, finances of governments and the global economy. A number of unethical and short-sighted leadership decisions of financial firms led to national and international instability. The search for ethical and sustainable leadership behavior has witnessed a substantial revival since then. Employees are looking for leaders who will create current and future profits for organizations; leaders who strive for improving the lives of many and not only securing the prosperity of few. Corporate social responsibility, corporate citizenship, corporate governance and sustainable leadership will thus become more relevant for leaders. In this respect it has become more obvious that sustainable success depends not only on the shareholder, but also on all (other) relevant stakeholders of an organization, including customers, shareholders, employees and society.

Sustainable leadership is another concept which organisations must consider, alongside sustainable and knowledge-based value that generates revenue.

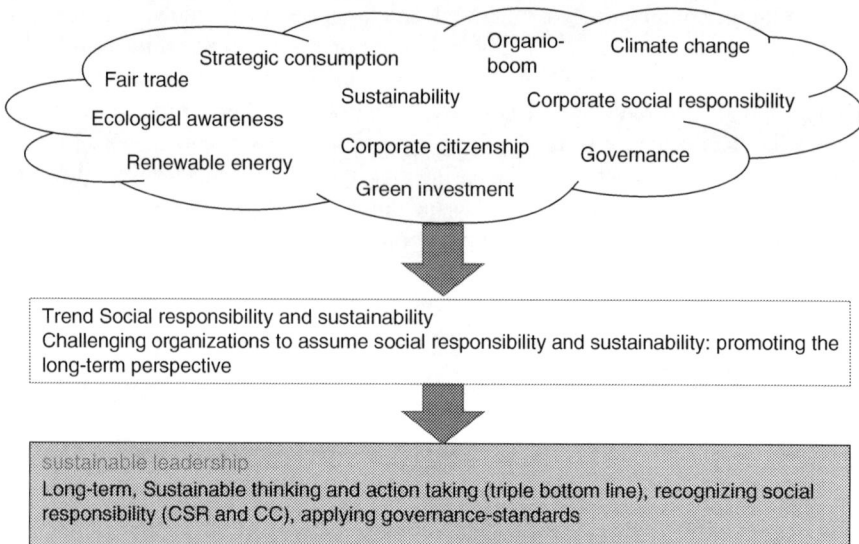

Fig. 1.5 Summary of trend Social Responsibility and Sustainability

"**Sustainable leadership**" is rooted in the idea that business strategies combine a concern for environmental, societal and economic issues. The World Commission on Environment and Development, founded by the United Nations in 1983, was the first commission to highlight the issue of "social responsibility" in addition to economic and ecological interests, expanding the responsibility of businesses. The Brundtland Report on sustainable development defines the term sustainable as "meeting the needs of the present generation without compromising the ability of future generations to meet their needs" (WCED, United Nations, 1987, p. 43).

Sustainable business discourses focus on 'triple bottom line' (Elkington, 1998) outcomes, in which business strategies should be socially and environmentally responsible as well as economically profitable. Business strategies aiming at balancing all three orientations – people, planet and profits – (Elkington, 1998) need to be highly flexible and adaptable (Fig. 1.5).

"Sustainable leadership" pays tribute to the inevitable dynamics of social and ecological systems by providing clear direction but enough flexibility to allow for course corrections. Sustainable leadership identifies multiple stakeholders and their demands towards the organization. After a considerate evaluation of the involved interests, the social and ecological impact of leadership decisions will be evaluated and integrated in economic decision making processes.

Different concepts are built on the assumption of extended business responsibility of companies. This includes:

- The concept of sustainable development with its triple bottom line
- The concepts of Corporate Social Responsibility with the extension into the social dimension of business responsibility or
- Corporate Citizenship, where the company behaves like a good citizen

1.7 Trend 5: Social Responsibility and Sustainability

In sum, different concepts cover enlarged business responsibility towards multiple stakeholders (CSR, sustainable growth) as an essential strategy to secure sustainable long-term economic and social growth. The quality and consequences of leadership decisions will be examined regarding their ecological and social impact. Leadership and HRM offer various opportunities to implement social responsibility and sustainability strategically. The aim is to achieve economic success, but not at the expense of the environmental and social impact, and with the active use of these effects for the company's success. Leadership and HRM offer several options to strategically implement social and sustainable responsibility. The most diverse international legal norms and economic commitments identify action fields for the design of employee relationship and leadership, and can be summarized in the following fields of action (see Eberhardt, 2010, 2013c):

1. Putting a strategic and normative focus on sustainability and social responsibility
   This field of action deals with stakeholders' interests, HR philosophy, HR strategy and company's values.
2. Enabling a balanced HR demography and diversity
   HR demography and diversity considers as possible courses of action the heterogeneous composition of workers in the organization. Equal treatment and diversity are central issues.
3. Hiring and keeping employees long-term
   This field of action deals with aspects of HR marketing, recruitment, employee protection laws, opportunities of career development and performance management.
4. Implementing leadership and cooperation collaboratively
   Here, the action deals with the formation of follower relations from the line manager's perspective. Cooperative leadership involves followers 'engagement, the promotion and development of employees' and supervisors' skills. Value driven leadership prevents mobbing, discrimination and other stressful working relations.
5. Supporting participation in decision-making processes
   Collective participation rights, in terms of access to information and participation, are central themes of action five. Advisory or supervisory boards, trade unions and independent employee organizations are central aspects. A further essential theme relates to transparent information management.
6. Promoting learning
   This action domain contains all forms of lifelong learning, e.g., personal development, career development and further education opportunities offered on, and off the job.
7. Wage differentiation
   Action domain seven deals with a differentiated handling of wages. Differentiated pay secures social security and performance orientation. Minimum wages, wage differentiation, the implementation of wage transparency and adequate wage ranges are possible courses of action.

8. Work security and health management

    This action domain considers work procedures and habits which promote good health, health management and work security (including prevention of accidents).
9. Enabling compatibility of "life domains"

    "Life-Domain" includes concepts which encourage a balanced work and private life. Various part-time work models and family support systems are examples of this action domain.
10. Ensuring work and employability

    Action ten puts a focus on HR practices, which sustain the employability of workers.

Chapter 2
Study "Think Tank: The Future of Leadership"

> *Traditionally leaders have thought that the way to learn to be better leaders is to look at other leaders for what worked. Instead leaders are going to have to start asking themselves 'why would anybody want to follow me'?* (Carole Robin)

The explorative interview study was conducted with 20 leadership experts. The aim of "Think Tank: The Future of Leadership" was to reflect on the impact of major future trends on leadership. The experts evaluated how important societal, social and economic trends affect organizations, employees and leadership practices. In this context, as experts gave insights into their own leadership visions, they also started questioning which leadership skills are beneficial and what it takes to give leaders the strength to tackle future challenges.

The surveyed experts are managers, professors, trainers and consultants, who can draw on many years of professional experience in these roles. The interviewees were from San Francisco Bay Area and Silicon Valley. This area is also characterized as an "innovation capital" (see Piscione, 2013), and is known for highly innovative companies which enable innovative projects in rapid innovation cycles. One interviewee lives in Switzerland and has been in a leadership position for several decades himself. During this time he shaped the leadership development in Switzerland, set future-oriented topics and made them available in executive training practice. The findings from the present interview study from Silicon Valley are aimed at providing impetus for the European Economic Area with a focus on Germany and Switzerland. In particular, the economically strong countries at the heart of Europe with their political stability, high export orientation, high education standards, high innovation potential and exemplary low unemployment rate are some of the most attractive business locations in the Western world. To ensure innovative economic development in Germany and Switzerland, it is necessary to consider the future needs of leadership and to reflect on the related question of how leaders can address these challenges.

A total of 25 h and 19 min of interview recordings were transcribed and qualitatively evaluated. On average, the key themes of the interview were dealt within

1½–2 h. The first couple of interviews were held using a detailed interview manual. To prevent exceeding the scheduled interview time, the following interviews were based on an abridged interview questionnaire (see Sect. 2.5.2).

2.1 Descriptive Characteristics of the Interview Partners

The following section summarizes main descriptive characteristics of the interview partners such as current professional role, prior education, career and leadership experience.

2.1.1 Current Professional Role

Six interview partners indicated their current roles to be entrepreneurs, consultants and lecturers. Five interviewees were leaders of a company or a business unit. A number of interview partners described their professional roles as involving more than one profession, for instance, four respondents act as both consultants and lecturers (see Fig. 2.1).

2.1.2 Prior Education

A large number of interviewees hold an educational background in economics (e.g., BA, strategic management or operation). The second major part of the sample reported a technical (IT/engineering) or scientific educational background.

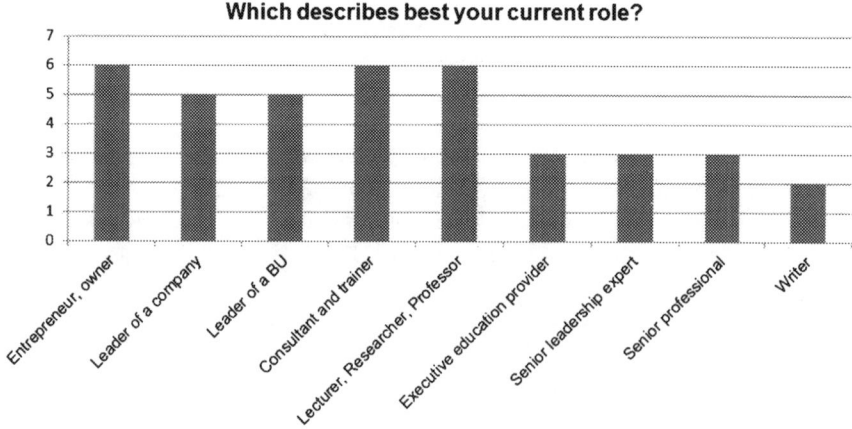

Fig. 2.1 Current role

2.2 Method

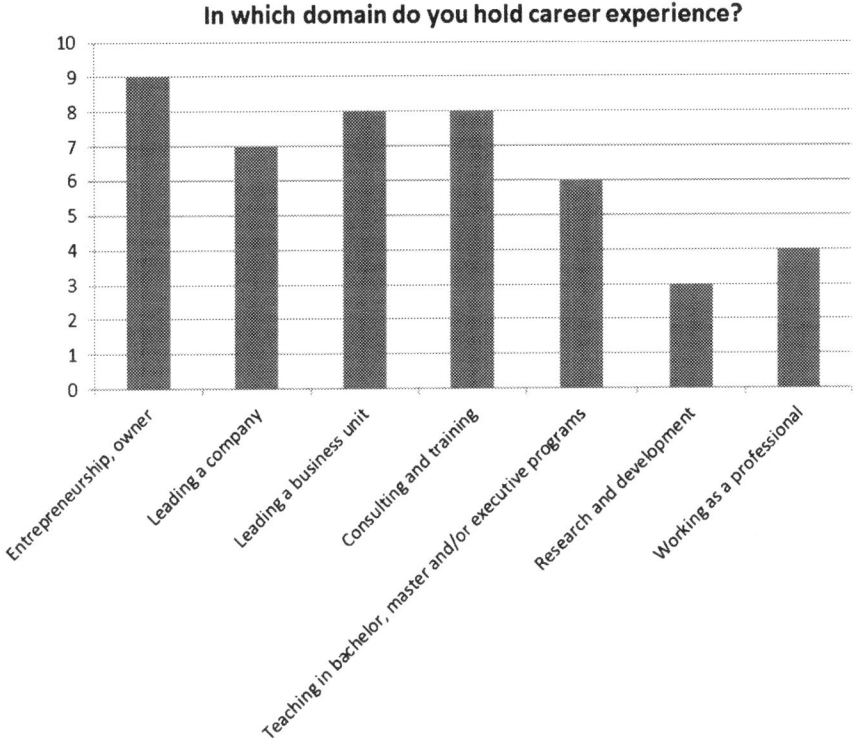

Fig. 2.2 Career experience

2.1.3 Career Experience

Figure 2.2 displays the career domains in which the interview partners gathered professional experience. Most of the respondents who worked as entrepreneurs (7 out of 9) also have experience in leading a company. The respondents who have experience in teaching and research have also mostly worked as consultants (5 out of 9).

Analyzed by industry sectors the results show a wide range, with clusters in the high-tech (5 out of 20), education (5 out of 20) and consulting sectors (4 out of 20) (see Fig. 2.3).

2.2 Method

The following section describes the methodological approach of content based qualitative analysis. The authors are aware that the posed interview questions were broadly defined and that consequently any systematic analysis of the interviews will

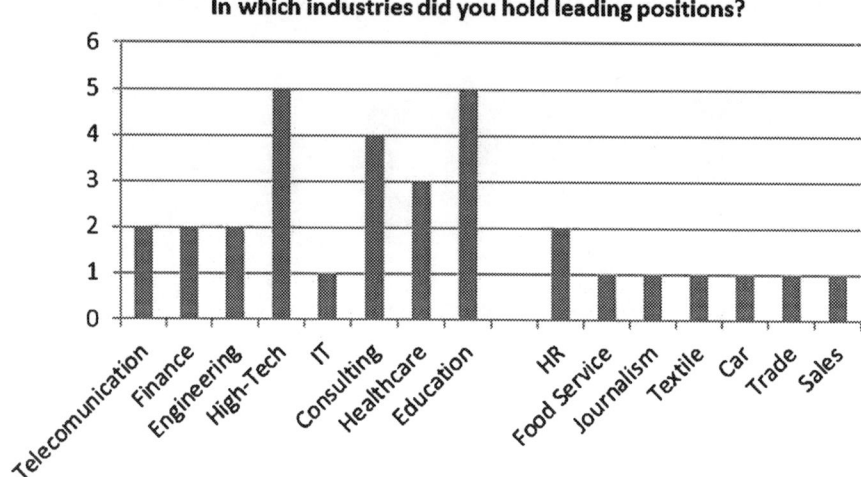

Fig. 2.3 Leading positions (industries)

result in broader summaries of the individual statements. The content based analysis and developed coding scheme mainly strived to capture the diversity of the perspectives on future leadership trends, paying tribute to the heterogeneous richness of the inputs from the leadership experts. The inclusion of individual quotes aims at mirroring the diversity of thoughts and statements and to exemplify the respective statements.

2.2.1 Development of the Coding Scheme

The interview data were analyzed using qualitative content analysis according to Mayring (2010). The interviews were recorded and subsequently transcribed verbatim following predefined rules. A coding scheme, comprised deductive and inductive methods, was developed. On one hand, the codes for the five future trends were derived theoretically, taking into account the explorative research question of the study, as suggested by the five leadership trends. On the other hand, themes were identified from the script, paying tribute to the explorative nature of the study, which allows themes to be identified from the scripts. The initial coding scheme was established based on one selection criteria, striving to capture general, but person-specific, statements related to the future of leadership including leadership challenges, leadership styles, roles, tasks, expectancies and coping mechanisms. As the contexts of the statements were relevant, thematic units were used, as opposed to line by line coding. A first version of the coding scheme was discussed by the researchers,

2.2 Method

Table 2.1 Summary of main categories

1	Personal current challenges as consultants and academics in teaching future leaders (e.g. MBA students, coaching clients)
2	Personal current challenges as a leader/manager
3	Elements which strengthen the interviewee in his or her role as a consultant/HE provider
4	Elements which strengthen the interviewee in his or her role as a leader/manager
5	The respective future trends and associated challenges, development opportunities and important competencies for leaders
6	Elements which strengthen leaders in mastering the challenges of the respective future trends
7	Impact of the demographic change on leader's roles and tasks
8	Ways of increasing women's participation rate in top management positions
9	Potential consequences of an increased level of women's participation rate in top management positions
10	Future essential skills/competencies and future essential characteristics (e.g., traits, behavioural tendencies) for followers

ambiguities were clarified and modifications of the coding scheme were carried out. The coding of the first 15 % of the material was conducted by one researcher, resulting in the definition of the initial categories. Next, two trial codings of two interviews were conducted independently by the two coders. When consecutively comparing the coding of the two transcripts only two minor discrepancies were found. The research team recoded the two trial interviews after having clarified the discrepancies. The research team then proceeded to establish intercoder reliability (ICR). The coding scheme for the establishing intercoder reliability consisted of 10 major categories (see Table 2.1) partially divided into subcategories to give a total of 42 subcategories. Two transcripts which had not been coded before were then independently coded by the two researchers, to establish consistency in their coding. Concordances and disconcordances of the two coders were recorded. A coding was regarded as concordant if both coders assigned the selected text passage to the same category.

Between the two researchers, agreement of an overall Cohen's kappa for all ten categories was calculated. Cohen's kappa relates the number of concordant ratings to the number of discordant ratings while taking into account the number of ratings that could be expected by chance. Cohen's kappa can yield values between −1 and +1. A value of +1 indicates absolute agreement among the coders. A value of 0 indicates an agreement purely by chance. Values below 0 indicate an agreement less likely than chance. According to Everitt (1996), kappa values between .41 and .60 can be regarded as moderate and values above .60 as satisfactory or solid agreements. The overall obtained kappa coefficient for the current study was .75, indicating a solid agreement between the two coders. The remaining 16 transcripts were subsequently coded by one researcher.

2.3 Results

The following result section displays the condensed findings of the qualitative content analyses. First an initial summary of the experts' description of their current work and leadership challenges and indication of the sources of strengths supporting the interview partners in their respective professional roles will be displayed. Next, the findings regarding the five future leadership trends of: Individualization, Transition to Flexibility, Demography, Rapid Social and Economic Changes and Social Sustainability and Responsibility will be reported. The presentation of the content analysis will start with a short summary of the main interview statements, and then be followed by the display of all main statements in table form. The main category headings will be provided as guiding headlines in the respective tables. Condensed interview statements listed in bold indicate that a minimum of two participants, and a maximum of four, highlighted this particular aspect.

2.3.1 Current Leadership, Career and Work Challenges

The first section of the interview asked the participants to describe their current leadership and work challenges. For the *consultants and academics* the challenge of broadening personal leadership images, such as leadership equals provision of definite answers, were picked up as central themes. Another emerging topic was the necessity to manage oneself effectively. As consultants, the interviewed experts emphasized the need to identify personal strengths and unique contributions in their consultancy practice. A final crucial element the interviewed consultants and academics are confronted with is providing a clear vision which inspires other people to drive towards that vision (Table 2.2).

For the interviewed *managers*, daily leadership challenges addressed during the interviews were recruiting top talent which represents a cultural and professional fit to the company. Creating cooperative, trusting and transparent organizational and working environments was a second leadership requirement being raised. "Intercultural leadership" due to an increasingly diverse workforce was mentioned as one central challenge. The managers reported that heightened levels of intercultural sensitivity represent an essential managerial skill. In leading cross-cultural teams they need to demonstrate an awareness and acceptance for intercultural differences. Efficient personal and team management in view of high work pressure was another dimension raised by the managers (Table 2.3).

Table 2.2 Summary of current work and leadership challenges as consultants and HE providers

Personal current challenges as consultants and academics in teaching future leaders (e.g. MBA students, coaching clients)
Broadening common leadership images
Broadening MBA students' and clients' perspectives of personal mental leadership models, i.e. leaders do not need to provide all answers, instead leaders need to ensure that the best answers are found through asking the right questions
Increasing leader's awareness that the image of the perfect leader does not exist
Self-management skills
Leading oneself
Introspective views of personal strengths and unique contributions as a consultant
Being authentic and finding one's voice
Providing vision and direction
Identifying your personal vision and goals which will inspire other people to drive towards that vision
Sharing a vision for creating high integrity leadership
Providing direction in fragmented environments

Table 2.3 Summary of personal current work and leadership challenges as a leader/manager

Personal current challenges as a leader/manager
Recruiting top talent
Building a team and recruiting people who would be a good cultural and professional fit to the company
Selling ones passion and credibility to convince top employees to join your company
Creating an organizational culture ensuring cooperation and beneficial communication patterns
Creating an organizational culture of openness and transparency
Creating an organizational culture characterized by flat hierarchies and open communication channels
Creating transparent working procedures to ensure mutual cooperation
Building trust in a team: employees should trust in leader's competencies and support
Keeping long-term perspective in complex environments
Figuring out long-term development given different costumer requests
Trying to see clarity in taking the right actions in a fragmented environment such as complex markets
Intercultural leadership
Dealing with an increasingly diverse workforce (i.e. people from different educational backgrounds, different nationalities and different skill sets)
Demonstrating awareness for intercultural differences
Depending on geographical location, the need to adapt to employees' different personalities, to different structures and social costumes
Working with a global workforce: managing geographical distances and different time zones
Creating awareness that acceptance of one's own leadership varies depending on cultural context
Organizational and time management skills while providing the vision of a leader
Ensuring efficient personal and team time management
Coping with high workload
Setting priorities
Being a good leader *and* a good manager; acting as a role model who provides a vision and demonstrating operational competencies

Table 2.4 Summary of elements which strengthen the interviewees as consultant/HE providers

Elements which strengthen the interviewee in his or her role as a consultant/HE provider
Congruency and consistency in personal convictions and teaching consulting practices
Philosophical and socio-critical contemplations considering one's role and responsibilities as a consultant
Supervisor's support
Keeping a personal journal of reflections on successful and unsuccessful behaviors
Identifying what intrinsically motivates people
Faith and belief
Family support
Being independent of social judgments
Academic freedom

2.3.2 What Strengthens Leaders in Their Leadership Roles?

The next section of the interview asked the interviewees to identify elements which improve the execution of their respective roles. For the interviewed *academics and consultants*, one central source of strength was related to ensuring congruency and consistency in personal values and convictions and teaching/consultancy practices. Other sources of support being identified were being able to count on supervisor's support, identifying what truly motivates people and academic freedom. The following table summarizing all main statements related to elements strengthening the interviewed consultants and professors/lecturers in their professional roles (Table 2.4).

For the interviewed *managers*, different interpersonal skills such as listening, patience and the ability to identify and maximise employees' strengths while minimizing weaknesses, were identified as sources of strength. Additional support elements of effective leadership roles were ensuring a healthy work life balance through regular exercise and healthy nutrition. The managers reported a number of leadership styles, competencies and characteristics which support them in their daily practice, such as applying intuition in decision making processes, high stress tolerance, accepting trial and error in certain development processes and an openness towards experiencing new cultures and people. A final theme which was raised by the managers was being able to operate from a secure base. This meant being able to rely on supervisor's professional support and feeding from inner sources of energy coming from creative work or travelling (Table 2.5).

2.4 Trend 1: Individualization

> *Leadership is going to become more and more about being good at influencing others.*
> (Carole Robin)

Table 2.5 Summary of elements which strengthen the interviewees as leaders/managers

Elements which strengthen the interviewee in his or her role as a leader/manager
Different facets of interpersonal skills
Listening skills
Patience
Finding people's strengths and minimizing their weaknesses
Building personal relationships with team members, which are built on mutual trust and respect
Compassion for others
Setting boundaries while demonstrating high levels of stress tolerance
Demonstrating high stress tolerance
Ensuring work-life balance: staying health and exercising regularly
Strictly setting boundaries between work and private life
Particular leadership styles and characteristics strengthening leaders in their daily practice
Intuition
Being authentic
Not being too political aggressive and reaching for power
Not trying to be good at something you are not good at
Accepting a more pragmatic way of trial and error instead of expecting perfection from the start
Applying bottom-up leadership processes
Setting conditions which will drive other people
Openness to experience, new cultures and people
Risk management
Taking personal risks such as risking personal reputation when stating opinions
A secure base: falling back on strong personal principles and relying on external support
Supervisor's professional and moral support
A secure base: trust in your supervisor to openly exchange professional views given the increasing amount of complexity
Inner source of energy: family, own creative work, travelling and nature
Strong value orientation
Strong sense of identity

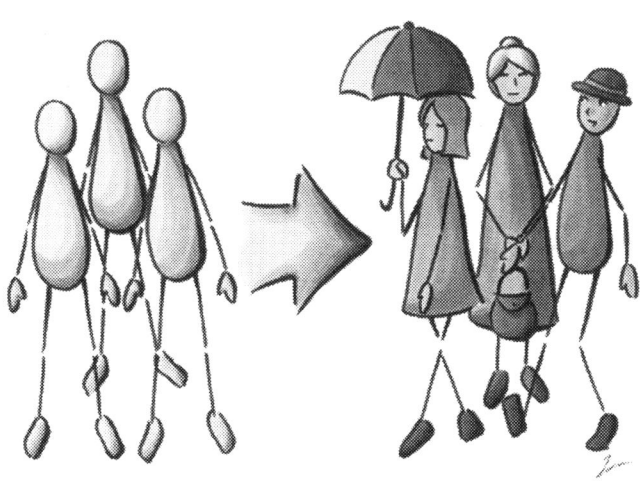

Note: The graphic representations of the respective listed trends were created by Jana Eberhardt.

2.4.1 Leadership Style: "Personal Leadership"

> *I mean you have to focus on the individual and each individual is different, each individual has a different package.* (Ajay Bam)

The following section describes the condensed findings with regard to the Individualization trend and its proposed associated leadership styles, described by the term "personal leadership". As a result, future predictions regarding the onset of the "personal leadership" trend were suggested. While a number of interviewees suggested Individualization to be a growing trend in the future, other voices indicated that future organizations will not profoundly change to consider the individuals needs of their employees. As a consequence a growing mismatch between employees' expectations and their workplace demands will occur. Further predictions related to varying generation specific expectancies. For instance, younger generations express more boldly their needs regarding alternative work models and working arrangements. A further leadership challenge which was raised by the interviewees was concerned with gaining employees' trust and dealing with heterogeneous expectations. Leaders will increasingly need to deal with employees changing their employer more frequently; keeping employees long-term and motivated thus represents a challenge. Especially when managing highly skilled workers, leaders need to focus more on the individual employee. Further leadership requirements which were suggested with regard to "personal leadership" were moving away from a "one size fits all approach" to leadership. The focus on "unique individuals" and teams in individualized leadership was particularly raised by the interviewees. This leadership approach necessitates a leader's openness towards soft skill development. An appreciation for diverse teams is encouraged for the future and team members' strengths should be identified and leveraged. In this respect, future leaders need to demonstrate coaching and mentoring abilities in order to cope with the trend of Individualization (Table 2.6).

We can try to summarize all these growing needs for "personal leadership" with the following quota:

> *We are going to need more leadership style that includes emotional intelligence or capacity to relate.* (Chris Sablynski)

2.4.2 Leadership Style: "Co-leadership"

> *Planning skills, communicating skills, I think sometimes the problem with co-leadership is everybody thinks the other person is doing it and then nobody does it.* (David Eu)

With regard to the "co-leadership", the interview partners predicted an increase in this particular leadership style due to a decrease in centralized structures. Further predictions were that instead of one leader there will be "leadership within a team". Leaders dealing with this particular future leadership style should hold a diverse network which can quickly be activated when needed. Leaders will need to work

2.4 Trend 1: Individualization

Table 2.6 Summary of leadership style: "Personal leadership"

Future predictions
Individualization as a growing trend in the future
The future will hold contradictory trends: on one hand a stronger emphasis on the individual, while on the other a trend towards standardized employees
Despite current debates there is no evidence that organizations have changed in the last 5–10 years and will not profoundly change to consider the individuals needs and expectations of their employees. However, if given a change in employees' individual expectancies, an increasing mismatch between employees and their workplace demands will occur. As a consequence, leaders will need to deal with decreased levels of job satisfaction of their employees
The language of HRM will not be a language of individuation: "The language of human capital, the language of human resources"
Individualization and associated challenges, development opportunities and important competencies for leaders
Individualization and associated expectations from an employees' perspective
Different generational expectations: Younger employees expect more flexibility at work (e.g., working remotely)
Talented individuals will not look primarily for monetary incentives, but will place value on personal and professional development and a sense of ownership at work
Followers will increasingly expect to be taken seriously
"Personal leadership" requires coaching and mentoring abilities
Leadership is not a one size fits all approach. It has to be individualized and customized with respect to each employee (e.g. the unique ways in which employees learn and process information)
Leaders need to treat individuals as unique and not dispensable
To secure extraordinary talent in the organization leaders have to focus on the individual and each individual has a different package
The leader of the future is more of a director, controller or coach
Developing people instead of just leading people will become more important
"Personal leadership" requires essential soft skills as future essential skills
Leadership skills related to emotional intelligence, the capacity to relate, empathy, honesty and personal appeal
The need for soft skill development
Leaders need to be aware how their behaviour and communication patterns affect people
Leaders need to gain the trust of their employees
Leaders are encouraged to develop an appreciation for differences in their team members, as well as leveraging their individual strengths

with partners and competitors at the same time, and in alternating roles. Leaders are thus encouraged to be flexible in their personal leadership style, depending on the work relations. It will be essential for future leaders to unite people who hold essential information whilst keeping the "big picture". The question of which elements strengthen leaders in view of the trend Individualization highlighted soft skills such as emotional intelligence and increased awareness of how one's own personal leadership behaviour and communication style affects other people. Additional points raised were the importance of active listening and posing the right question to

Table 2.7 Summary of leadership style: "Co-leadership"

Future predictions
The "co-leadership" trend will be of increasing importance in the future
As there is a breakdown of centralized structures, the future world requires "co-leadership". Instead of one leader there will be "leadership within a team"
"Co-leadership" and associated challenges, development opportunities and important competencies for leaders
In view of increasing interdependencies leaders need to learn how to negotiate mutual benefits
Leaders need to be able to relate to people and hold a diverse network which can be activated quickly when needed
Leaders should not only have networks and connections, they should to be able to work with competitors and partners at the same time
"Co-leadership" necessitates flexible adaptation of leadership practices
Leaders will be challenged when confronted with employees holding different levels of information. Leaders will have to connect the people holding the essential information while keeping the overall picture

Table 2.8 Summary of elements which strengthen the interviewees in relation to the trend individualization

What will strengthen leaders mastering the challenges associated with the trend Individualization?
Practicing emotional intelligence
The ability to compromise
Active listening, open and respectful behavior and posing the right questions
Accepting employees' individuality
Talent attraction and retention; "the work itself has to be fun"
Being involved in many facets of the company while also allowing employees to lead their parts
Acting as facilitators who set up conditions and systems enabling the employees to reach their goals

retrieve relevant information. A central theme being raised related to the ability to compromise and the capacity to accept employees' individuality. The ability to compromise and the acceptance of individuality in standardized working conditions will strengthen leaders in dealing with individualised social and working structures (Tables 2.7 and 2.8).

To be successful in different ways of "co-leadership", interaction and communication is crucial. It further requires the ability to establish a favourable environment and to work flexibly with others. Ideas for the future of interaction and communication are the following:

> *The future questions will have to be more humble, because you can't build a trusting relationship if you don't accept a certain amount of humility and vulnerability vis-à-vis the other person. For me to seek your help and ask you questions and get interested in you makes me vulnerable. And I will only do that if I recognize if I'm the leader that I am dependent on you to some degree. That creates the humility (…) if the leader makes himself vul-*

2.5 Trend 2: Transition to Flexibility

nerable to the subordinate that elicits positive feelings and trust, so we are getting down to very fundamental things in the culture (Edgar Schein)
   So leadership is really being able to connect to other people and to find and elicit and catalyze greatness through an effective interaction. (Jeannie Kahwajy)

2.5 Trend 2: Transition to Flexibility

For a leader it is very important to be able to handle the balance between experimentation and focus. (Gioia Deucher)

2.5.1 Leadership Style: "Liquid Leadership"

Networks – the ability to connect these LEGO's who each individually make sense, but if you bring them together it makes bigger sense. (Frederic Mauch)

The following section displays the findings regarding of Transition to Flexibility trend and its proposed associated leadership styles, such as "liquid leadership". Future leadership challenges being addressed during the interviews related the provision of orientation in increasingly liquid economic and social structures. The management of decentralized teams demands clear management by objectives and specifications of expectancies. Leaders should expect well-informed employees due to the democratization and availability of information. Another future leadership challenge which was brought up by the interview partners in relation to "liquid leadership" saw followers more energized as a result of communicating directly with their leaders thanks to technical developments such as twitter and other social medial platforms. The emergence of flat hierarchies needs to be accepted at

Table 2.9 Summary of leadership style: "Liquid leadership"

"Liquid leadership" and associated challenges, development opportunities and important competencies for leaders
Providing a sense of orientation in increasingly liquid structures
Leaders need to give orientation
The individual has a need for continuity and orientation
Leaders need to become more of a mentor and a navigator, who helps employees build their own networks
Leading teams remotely in virtual environments, leaders have to set clear goals and expectations while simultaneously trusting employees to do their jobs
Leaders need to be able to develop a common team identity
Providing a vision for the future
Leaders need to know what they stand for and should be the ones defining the values of the company
A key issue for leaders is to provide a vision for the future
The liquidation of systems and its impact on leader-follower-relations
The liquidation of systems and increased approachability of leaders due to technical developments (i.e. twitter) will encourage followers to communicate directly with leaders
Leaders are encouraged to adapt to more flat hierarchies
An increase in online relationships increases the need for shared face-to-face experience
Leaders need to create positive interactions and positive shared experiences

leadership level. However, despite the rapid increase in online relationships, the need for face-to-face encounters will simultaneously be intensified (Table 2.9).

The liquidation of systems is limited if it comes towards leading employees. They still will act according to their personal resources:

> Some individuals are very self-driven. Some individuals need to be micromanaged and told step-by-step what to do and if you have different types of individuals you have to create an environment where they are successful. (T. M. Ravi)

2.5.2 Leadership Style: "Complexity Leadership"

> Try, fail, restart, try is upmost, it's a management process and we do it quite frequently. (Ken Mooyman)

Leaders of the future will operate in an environment of increasing complexity and uncertainty. Data management and statistical knowledge will be of increasing importance. Given the unpredictability and complexity of new emerging markets, the strategy of try, error and retry was identified as one useful strategy

2.5 Trend 2: Transition to Flexibility

to test ideas. As the different industry sectors undergo regular changes, management and business strategies need to be monitored and adapted at regular intervals.

To deal with increased levels of complexity, the interview partners suggested the following leadership skills and styles as resourceful management strategies: acting as a mentor and navigator for the employees in building up their networks. Leaders should be responsive and supportive role models. In dealing with large amount of complex data, leaders should avoid being trapped and feeling overwhelmed by large amounts of data. Instead, by asking the right questions, leaders can identify and retrieve essential information. The process of introducing post decision evaluations allows leaders to be more flexible in response to changing markets and economic challenges (Tables 2.10 and 2.11).

Table 2.10 Summary of leadership style: "Complexity leadership"

Future perspectives
Being able to analyse complex situations represents an essential future competency for leaders
Data management and statistical knowledge will be increasingly important in the future
To operate in an environment of increasing complexity and uncertainty will be an essential future leadership task
The drive to implement big data management tools will increase
"Complexity leadership" and associated challenges, development opportunities and important competencies for leaders
"Try, fail and restart" as one strategy to deal with increasing levels of complexity
In dealing with increasing levels of complexity, try, error and retry has become a successful strategy in certain industries
Leaders need to provide followers the chance to test new ideas. However, the process of try and fail needs to happen in a limited time frame to avoid companies wasting valuable resources
Proposed strategies of dealing with complex big data sets
"Big Data" can create a trap in the decision making process: data can support decision-making, but can also paralyze it due to an oversupply of information
To think like scientists: intellectual curiosity as a drive for development
The ability to pose the right questions given complex and contradictory information
Leaders need to pose the right questions and develop defence mechanisms to prevent being overwhelmed by big data; decision making quality does not improve with increasing availability of information
Enabling employees to formulate goal orientated questions
Initiation of post-decision evaluations
As the market and industry continuously change, there is no one best approach to management. Management strategies will need to be adapted and monitored at regular intervals

Table 2.11 Summary of elements which strengthen the interviewees in relation to the trend transition to flexibility

What will strengthen leaders mastering the challenges associated with the transition to flexibility trend?
Implementing the right HR policies and HR tools to facilitate liquid organization and flexible working patterns
Establishing a positive reputation
Being cooperative
Being self-confident
Setting clear protocols for behavioural respectful leadership conduct
Acting as role models

With all the discussions about the availability of big data and the fact that "great leadership decisions" are always based on lots of data, we would like to present the following quotes:

> *I am suggesting that data is not the only element in the decision. It informs the decision but it doesn't make the decision.* (Larry Robertson)
>
> *I think there is an issue of focus with all of these new communication technologies. Everybody checking their Facebook page every minute or their e-mail has made focus much more difficult. So it's become a difference in degree rather than kind, but the leaders still need to keep people focused on what they need to be doing, and the people need to keep themselves focused of what they need to be doing.* (Jeffrey Pfeffer)

2.6 Trend 3: Demography

> *If you are not taking the best elements and best resources that are available you are hurting your own ability to run a great organization. You're limiting yourself. And so that is kind of a mistaken notion that homogeneity can kind of help reduce friction and that's good, but that's not really the case if you want a high performing organization.* (T.M. Ravi)

2.6 Trend 3: Demography

2.6.1 Leadership Style: "Age-Related Leadership"

> *I think experience really matters so I think you would want to keep your more experienced sales people healthy and not burned out, so that they want to stay on and train the newer generation.* (Kate Sherwood)

The following section describes the condensed findings with regard to the Trend Demography and its proposed associated "age-related leadership" style.

The relevant qualitative analyses revealed a number of proposed impacts of the demographic change on leader's roles and tasks. The interview partners reported different generational skill-sets to be affecting leadership practices. For instance, senior leaders need to utilise the knowledge advantages of their younger employees. In this respect, leaders should strive to benefit from the age-specific strengths of the younger generation and benefit from "digital-natives". "Age-related leadership" will increasingly require sensitivity trainings on diversity issues. Significant age differences in the leader-follower relationship demand clarification of expectancies and implicit assumptions. Leaders are in demand to enable positive encounters for different age groups. As diverse work teams are increasingly becoming high performance teams, leading cross-generational teams will be an essential future leadership challenge (Table 2.12).

Table 2.12 Summary of leadership style: "Age-related leadership"

Impact of the demographic change on leader's roles and tasks
Different generational skill sets
Differences in technical skill capacities: A young CEO might be much happier blogging/tweeting experiences by the minute while some 70 year-old CEOs have never written an email before
Leaders need to embrace the technological advantage held by younger employees
Leaders need to use the strengths of the different age groups (e.g. "digital natives" covering the aspect of new communication technologies and social media)
Diversity sensitivity training, clarifying assumptions and harnessing the strengths of cross generational team members
Sensitivity training on diversity issues will be a growing trend in the next 15 or 20 years
If significant age differences exist between leaders and their employees, assumptions and expectations need to be clarified in the leader-follower relationship
As cross generational teams will be the high performance teams of the future, leaders need to guide cross-generational teams in identifying their strengths and weaknesses
Leaders need to provide different age groups the opportunity to cooperate and positively interact
Experience matters, therefore keeping older people to train the younger generation represents a key future task for leaders
HOWEVER: The majority of further education programmes do not provide any programs for the age group of 55+

2.6.2 Leadership Style: "Gender-Related Leadership"

I do think there is definitely a need for female leadership – for the specific strengths that women bring into leadership positions. (Gioia Deucher)

Given skilled workers shortage potentially hurting many labour markets, the future will hold for leaders the increasing social demand to introduce more widely inclusive initiatives. The internal attitude and organizational culture should support women in their career paths and provide them with relevant mentoring and networking support. In this respect, HR policies should be aimed at a gender-balanced workforce. Leaders supporting women in their career advancement should be gender neutral in identifying talent and conscious about recognizing gender dynamics at work. In particular, leaders should trust women with the same task as men. Female leaders should actively speak up and support the progress of other women's careers. The interview partners also mentioned that women themselves need to actively promote their own career prospects by making use of coaching and mentoring opportunities and by actively asking for promotion (Table 2.13).

"Gender-related leadership" and different perspectives on its implementation:

Table 2.13 Summary of leadership style: "Gender-related leadership"

Ways of increasing women's participation rate in top management positions
Organizational, social and governmental support to achieve women leadership
The internal attitude and culture of an organization should support women in their career paths
Creating mixed-gender work groups will create an appreciation of the opposite sex
Essential HR policies must be in place to ensure a gender balance in your workforce
Quotas as a tool to increase women's participation rate in top management positions
Impose the temporary rule of having three women board members
Governmental support is necessary to facilitate the balance between family and career
Social norms which support a different image of working women
Social norms should picture powerful women leaders as standard in the workplace
Career success should not be associated with being part of the "boys club"
Presently, role models demand women choose between family or career
Leaders supporting women in climbing the career ladder
Talent management should be gender neutral
Women should be trusted with the same tasks as men
Inclusive initiatives should become a genuine priority on a leader's agenda. Simply appointing a chief diversity officer will not be sufficient anymore
Women should receive strong mentoring support
Women taking the initiative in making a career
Women aiming to reach top management positions need to be able to mobilize their network and understand the relationship pieces underneath
Women should be encouraged to make use of coaching and mentoring support
The active use of support networks will be beneficial for career development
Female role models should speak up for other women

(continued)

2.6 Trend 3: Demography

Table 2.13 (continued)

Ways of increasing women's participation rate in top management positions
Women should take the initiative and not wait for their organizations to introduce inclusive diversity policies
Women are encouraged to actively ask for promotion; otherwise they will not be noticed
Learn from other female leaders
Female leaders will be strengthened by maintaining their individual identities and not strive to be somebody they're not
Female workers should be less questioning their abilities
Potential consequences of an increased level of women's participation rate in top management positions
Increased participation rate of women in top management positions suggested *making* a difference
Women are less aggressive in pursuing their point of view and more willing to take another person's perspective
Leadership is primarily about creating relationships with people. The female ability to understand emotions and people could thus make them better leaders
The female leadership style is typically more cooperative, communicative and integrative
Female leaders are better at adapting to diversity at the workplace, i.e. diversity of opinions and values
For women and men it is challenging to work for or with opposite sex supervisors, employees or colleagues. Egos in the workplace and attributed gender roles can impede professional working relations
Increased participation rate of women in top management positions suggested *not* making a difference
Leadership styles should be well suited to the business environment, irrespective of the sex of the leaders
Organizational filtering and socialization processes will produce male and female managers with similar characteristics and subsequently they will become almost indistinguishable in their leadership styles
Being authentic, moral and honourable represents a desirable leadership style, irrespective of the sex of the leader

I think women need to take care of themselves. They should stop waiting for the organizations to become more inclusive. (Jeffrey Pfeffer)

The first thing we need to do is help men become more aware of their privilege as men. It's not, that they are deliberately marginalizing women…. it's like if you are the fish in the water you don't realize that you are a fish in the water or that there is even water. You only know that if you happen to not be the fish in the water and you are having to learn to cope and adapt to living in the water when you are not a fish. (Carole Robin)

Further education programs, which reveal different leadership styles, to make them tangible and match them to female leaders. There are also women who favour a masculine leadership style, but they need to be given the opportunity to make their own experience with it and they need to be trusted with the same task as men. (Sabine Erlenwein)

The participation rate of women on all management levels, also on top management level, will rather increase, because this is an opportunity to fill this gap. And (…) one discovers women as a talent reserve. (C.D. Eck)

2.7 Trend 4: Rapid Social and Economic Changes

Top-down always is the only way you can begin a cultural change. (Edgar Schein)

2.7.1 Leadership Style: "Change Leadership"

The following section describes the condensed findings with regard to the Rapid Social and Economic Changes trend and its proposed associated leadership style "change leadership". Leaders will need to prepare a vision for the future which will guide their workforce through rapid social, political and economic changes. Leaders are encouraged to adopt flexible leadership styles according to economic, national and political changes. The analysis of inter-connections between and within social and economic systems will be an essential future leadership trait, according to the interview partners (Table 2.14).

Table 2.14 Summary of leadership style: "Change leadership"

"Change leadership" and associated challenges, development opportunities and important competencies for leaders
Developing a vision for the future
Leadership strategies need to be adjusted to rapid economic, national and political changes
Joined-up thinking

2.7.2 Leadership Style: "Intercultural Leadership"

> *We have become interconnected across cultures, across economies and the leader, who doesn't understand the different motivations of people from different cultures is not going to survive, and will not be the leaders who develop the next generation of leaders.* (Ed Chaffin)

As globalization becomes more prevalent, companies encounter greater cultural diversity within the workforce. Leaders will thus need to expand their cultural mindset and learn how to cooperate with people from various cultural and social backgrounds. Employees should be sent abroad to experience, and gain understanding of intercultural sensitivity and broaden their perspectives. Cross-cultural team-building should be encouraged and tools and expert knowledge should be provided to maximise the benefits of team diversity. Providing resources, and training on, intercultural sensitivity will be increasingly important (Table 2.15).

The following statements were made in relation to the question asking of how to strengthen leaders faced with the Rapid Social and Economic Changes trend. Leaders are encouraged to learn to live with, and anticipate, the effects of political trends, or new sets of environmental policies, which could affect their future business decisions. Remaining aware of current world affairs will help leaders to adjust their strategic decisions accordingly.

The interview partners suggested that following behavioural traits and leadership styles would support leaders in managing diversity in the workplace: Openness to experience and being globally aware. Diversity at various levels of the organization should be actively embraced. By developing awareness of people's cultural identities, leaders will be able to interpret and manage sensitive social dynamics in cross-cultural team work (Table 2.16).

"Intercultural leadership" must be taught in the appropriate setting, preferably not at home:

> *It's going to be important for whatever kind of leadership training in the future that intercultural aspects are a piece of it and maybe even require time spent abroad in a few different locations, so that you are able to challenge your assumptions.* (Laura Erickson)

2.8 Trend 5: Social Responsibility and Sustainability

> *I think it's being able to think in systems. I think that leaders are going to have to think of, they are trained very well to keep the boundary on the system of their company, what they have to see is that there are inputs and outputs that they are not used to considering.* (Cynthia Scott)

Table 2.15 Summary of leadership style: "Intercultural leadership"

"Intercultural leadership" and associated challenges, development opportunities and important competencies for leaders
Demonstrating intercultural competencies and facilitating cross-cultural working relations
Be willing to develop their cultural mind set and horizon
Connecting with people who are demographically/culturally/socially/economically different from them
Familiarize themselves with the cultural habits of their employees
Develop intercultural competence in leading employees by working abroad
Travelling to countries which are relevant for their work
Facilitate intercultural exchange, i.e. sending employees abroad
Encourage cross-cultural teambuilding

Table 2.16 Summary of elements which strengthen the interviewees in relation to the trend rapid social and economic changes

What will strengthen leaders mastering the challenges associated with the trend rapid social and economic changes?
Essential competencies and motivational orientations
Openness to experience
Gathering international experience
Demonstrating a global mind-set that can accommodate different cultures internally
Respecting differences and demonstrating the willingness to harness cross cultures differences
Being sensitive to cultural differences and celebrating them
Acknowledging how deeply cultures are embedded into people's identities will help leaders cope with a multi-cultural workforce
Increasing the organizations' awareness of the wide-reaching impact that diversity has on their organization

2.8.1 Leadership Style: "Sustainable Leadership"

The following section summarizes the findings regarding the Social Responsibility and Sustainability trend and the "sustainable leadership" style. As the European and American understanding of entrepreneurial vs. managerial leadership seem to differ substantially, the initial thematic differentiation could not be investigated in the course of the interviews. Hence, the "Entrepreneurial leadership vs. Managerial leadership" style was omitted from further analyses.

The interviewees stated that "sustainable leadership" challenges ranged from being genuinely committed to "sustainable leadership" to thinking systematically about how their decisions will affect various stakeholders and communities. "Sustainable leadership" needs to find a balance between social responsibility and profit. In practicing "sustainable leadership", however, leaders should demonstrate a genuine commitment to sustainable management. Increasing one's awareness of how individual leadership decisions will affect various systems, communities and stakeholders outside the organizational boundaries will be a central leadership challenge. Leaders will increasingly need to give into customers' wishes to "go green" (Table 2.17).

To engage in "sustainable leadership" the following statements demonstrate how to get started:

> At the end of the day you are not running a philanthropic organization, you're running a corporation that requires profit and I think that you need to balance that significant need with the need to be a good corporate citizen in whatever way you want to talk about it and so that involves social responsibility, it involves sustainability, it involves all those things and so I think what the leader needs is the ability to pursue that which allows this. (Larry Robertson)
>
> I think when leaders have personal experiences with sustainability, it gives them a much bigger respect for the need for sustainability. (Kate Sherwood)

Table 2.17 Summary of leadership style: "Sustainable leadership"

"Sustainable leadership" and associated challenges, development opportunities and important competencies for leaders
Every leader will be affected by issues of social responsibility and sustainability
Demonstrating a true commitment to "sustainable leadership" by integrating sustainable leadership practices in both their own, and in the company's daily practices
Acting as role models in practicing "sustainable leadership", e.g. introducing recycling in daily business routines
Improving their systematic thinking and consider the impact of their decisions outside their organization
Developing an understanding that they are part of a complex chain and how their leadership decisions affect internal and external stakeholders
Finding a balance between social responsibility and profitability

2.9 Challenges, Development Opportunities and Important Competencies for Future Leaders: Conclusions

Leadership is going to stay the same unless we decide for it to be different. And my question is who and when are we going to decide to make it different (which means to concomitantly reward it differently)? (Jeannie Kahwajy)

The final part of the interview focused on the interviewees' personal conclusions regarding the onset of the five postulated future megatrends. One central leadership challenge which was imminent for the interview partners related to operating in increasingly complex and rapidly changing environments. Leaders will need to prepare their workforce for fast-pace work environments which increasingly demand prioritizing skills. Leaders of the future will be mentors guiding their workforce through uncertainty, instability and change. Future leaders should demonstrate personal accountability, and be willing to take personal responsibility for their actions. Another important skill is the ability to adopt a new mindset in driving innovation: "Try, fail and restart" as a legitimate leadership and development tool. Further future leadership requirements relate to communicating a clear vision. Creating a sense of purpose and direction in fragmented and rapidly changing environments will be extremely important. Future leaders will face global ecological, economic and social challenges such as global warming or economic crises. To overcome leadership challenges of the future communication and listening skills will be of growing importance. Maintaining and developing hard skills such as technical and professional knowledge will be of equal relevance. Interviewees stressed that leaders should demonstrate a certain level of humility in posing questions and gathering knowledge from their employees. Consequently, leaders are encouraged to build trustful relationships with their employees and openly exchange essential information with them. Finally, future leaders will increasingly need to find a balance between integrating employees' voices in the decision making processes and the necessity to implement decisions top down (Table 2.18).

Finally it can be thought about the question if future leadership skills really need to be of a new quality or if leadership requires certain very essentials skills now and in the future:

I think human understanding. I think they need to understand other people aren't the same as they are (…) learn that your opinion may not be the same as somebody else's opinion and how to respect or understand or listen to somebody else's opinion. (David Eu)

I think leaders need skills, need to understand human motivation and human behavior and they need skills in organizational dynamics and one of the most important skills is the ability to see the world from another person's perspective. But that's not the new skill, that's an old skill. (Jeffrey Pfeffer)

2.10 Future Essential Skills for Followers

I think we need followers that want to grow into leaders who want to make a difference in the lives of the people they are asked to lead. (Ed Chaffin)

2.10 Future Essential Skills for Followers

Table 2.18 Summary of conclusions drawn: future leadership challenges

Future leadership challenges: conclusions drawn
Operating in increasingly complex and rapidly changing environments
Rapid innovation cycles
Fast-paced work environments
Increased levels of complexity: leaders will need to prioritize
Delivering tools to employees to deal effectively with more complex and fast changing environments
Demonstrating a willingness to continually update one's mental model about leadership
Anticipating political/economic trends or new environmental policies
Guiding and implementing change
Emergence of new business structures
Being willing to take risks
Being willing to take personal responsibility
Putting a stronger focus on innovation and holding a clear vision
Time and space for innovation
Long-term orientation
"Try, fail and restart" as a leadership tool for innovation
Being able to communicate a clear vision
Creating a sense of purpose, direction and aspiration
Global challenges
Globalized organizational structures
Leading various individuals in various cultures
Putting a stronger emphasis on soft skills
Opening people's minds to collaboration
Being compassionate
Building large networks
Practicing active listening skills
Leaders need to think less as individuals and more as part of a team
Communication skills, i.e. communicating ideas and expectations clearly
Leading an increasingly growing diverse working force (e.g. age, sex)
Being willing to understand and listen to other people's opinions
Maintaining and developing hard skills
Continuously updating your technical and professional knowledge
Demonstrating a certain level of humility
Humbly acknowledging that leaders are dependent on their employees to a certain degree
Building trusting relationships with their employees and allowing them to exchange essential information in critical situations
Asking the right questions and becoming familiar with the knowledge structure of their employees
Admitting mistakes
Leadership as a balancing act
The right balance between employee participation and management needs to be found
Finding a balance between the aggressiveness it needs to drive certain agendas and an open environment where everybody is able to collaborate and communicate
Enabling personal success *and* employees' success

Table 2.19 Summary of future essential skills for followers

Future essential skills, competencies and characteristics (e.g., traits, behavioural tendencies) for followers
Flexibility and adaptability
Be able to adapt to changing conditions and environments
Openness to innovation
Be willing to step outside their comfort zone
Be willing to experiment, change and help others to do the same
Holding a vision and seeing oneself as a leader
Having a passion for a vision
Fully support a leader's vision
An eagerness to grow
Having the vision to see oneself as a leader
Acting independently and responsibly
Independent thinking and problem solving
Being responsible and ethically accountable
Questioning standards, refusing bad treatment at work and holding leaders accountable
Be willing to reject bad treatment
Be willing to question more
Be critical and address any wrongdoing

When being asked to identify the essential skills, competencies and characteristics for followers the respondents identified a willingness to be flexible to change as one central future skill. Additional skills which were mentioned were having a passion for a vision. Future followers should act courageously and aspire to become a leader themselves. Future followers will need to act responsibly and ethically and will need independent problem-solving skills. Future followers should voice their critical opinions and hold their leaders accountable. Future followers should have the confidence to stand up and refuse bad treatment at work (Table 2.19).

Finally, the followers of the future should be treated like the independent adults that they are:

> *Yeah, so you have to give your employees the ability to try something, but you cannot insult and betray them and kick them out, then you are setting the wrong example…* (Ajay Bam)
>
> *Whether it's a female or male or young or old, you need people who also want to step up.* (Ken Mooyman)
>
> *We need people who can take on the wicked problems that seem unsolvable and wrestle with them in new ways and keep getting up every day and go back and do it again. So we need people who are strong and hardy.* (Cynthia Scott)

Chapter 3
Leadership of the Future: Everything Different or Same Old Same Old?

3.1 Personal Conclusion

> *The future of leadership is the ability to bring order into a system of constant disorder.*
> (Daniela Eberhardt)

Talking about the future makes you curious. Gathering ideas from leadership experts gives the impression of knowing exactly what's coming up next. A number of publications, speeches and notes are available about future megatrends as well as forecasts. Still, we do not know what the future will hold. While reflecting on megatrends and their impact on leadership, the future is already taking shape. A number of anticipated events will occur, others won't. The anticipation of future leadership challenges is based on the interviewed experts' wealth of experience, their diverse background in different disciplines and their practice with regard to leadership topics.

The purpose of this study was to provide "food for thought" on one's personal professional situation and discover ideas to shape the future of leadership. Based on interviews experienced leaders and leadership experts were interviewed regarding future developments in leadership, future leadership challenges and essential leadership skills.

3.2 What Remains?

Organizations are part of social and economic systems with a focus on the "bottom line". Given social and economic developments the issue of "The War for Talent" and highly qualified employees will be of strategic importance.

Humans have individual needs, expectations, wishes and competencies. Their experience and behavior affect the success of the company substantially and can be positively influenced by leadership practices and HRM, but can never be completely regulated.

Leadership will be about dealing with ambiguity and indissoluble situations and challenges, now and in the future. Leaders have to find a way that fits the organization, the employees' needs and her- or himself to lead authentically. And it requires passion, personal resources and essential leadership skills for practicing successful leadership in a sustainable way.

3.3 What Does the Future Hold?

"To be successful, you need to know how to lead diversity!" This statement might be the leadership credo of the future. The main conclusion shall be anticipated: The *most important and exciting leadership task* of the future will be to connect different people with diverse skills, expectations, resources, motivations, national origins, talents, sexes and ages together! And the most *important challenge* for the development as a leader will be resilience; to become more resilient in dealing with the pressure of dealing with increasing levels of diversity with regard to skills, expectancies, resources, motivations, nationalities, talent, age and gender.

Megatrends are large-scale changes with global reach on all aspects of life in the following decades. From this, conclusions for the management of diversity can be drawn!

Individualization Value systems, based on personal desires and goals, personal responsibility and self-determination are growing in industrialized nations. Simultaneously, companies are becoming more "individualized". The classic organizational structures are supplemented and replaced by new and different forms of cooperation. Depending on the task, or project, the individual worker will either act as an employee or find themselves in a management task. Organizations will have to face this challenge "as ever" but challenges in demographic changes will become more prevalent; for these reasons it will be important to attract talented people with diverse skills and potential. Traditional hierarchies will be increasingly rejected and organization networks will complement traditional organizational structures.

Diversity management describes the understanding of specific expectations and the implementation of individualized leadership practices, without being unfair or losing sight of corporate matters. Diversity management further entails the establishment of trust, the use of coaching and mentoring tools, movement in networks and flexible working forms and for leaders to demonstrate role flexibility (e.g. as facilitators, experts, directors etc.).

> *Leadership is going to become more and more about being good at influencing others.*
> (Carole Robin, responsible for leadership training at Stanford)

3.3 What Does the Future Hold?

Flexibility Flexible forms of organizing work and social networks such as LinkedIn, Xing or Facebook have a profound impact on relations inside and outside the organization and liquidate system boundaries. Employees are connected and informed in many ways and leaders need to provide orientation instead of information. These large networks lead to less reliability in relationships and less stable forms of cooperation. At the same time, data-led management decisions will be more common as a result of digital networking and the increased availability of datasets. Yet employees, and leaders, can only deal with a certain amount of ambiguity, quantity and complexity. People often make successful "gut decisions" based on intuition.

Diversity leadership means working together in virtual environments and with diversely connected and informed employees. Technological developments which enable faster, asynchronous and direct contact, require the leader-follower relationship to be redefined. Online relationships must be supplemented by direct and personal contact, to capture the diversity of human interaction and communication. Data management and statistical knowledge will become increasingly important as well as the clear communication of goals and expectations in complex virtual environments.

> *I think there is an issue of focus with all of these new communication technologies. Everybody checking their Facebook page every minute or their e-mail has made focus much more difficult. So it's become a difference in degree rather than kind, but the leaders still need to keep people focused on what they need to be doing, and the people need to keep themselves focused of what they need to be doing.* (Jeffrey Pfeffer, Professor Stanford University)

Demographic Development Demographic change creates generational diversity in companies, with a higher proportion of older employees, and a "war for talent" within the Millennials. There needs to be an examination of generation-specific needs, skills, working methods and attitudes. Bringing generations together means to meet the unique characteristics of the respective age groups and to simultaneously strengthen the cooperation across generations. Demographic development makes the increase of women in professional and managerial positions, also at top management level, more essential than ever. This requires a modified approach in dealing with role models and gender-based communication.

Leading diversity is concerned with the use of the specific characteristics and strengths of the respective ages and generations, to ensure the transfer of skills such as the use of digital media or long-standing experience and knowledge, and to promote intergenerational cooperation. Promoting health in the workplace, and lifelong learning ambitions, also count as diversity management tasks. Gender specific patterns in leadership and cooperation, the examination of promotion practices of women and men, the reconciliation of work and family life, the promotion of female role models and networking of women through mentoring and networking events are also facets of the management of diversity.

If you are not taking the best elements and best resources that are available you are hurting your own ability to run a great organization. You're limiting yourself. (TM Ravi, venture capitalist Palo Alto)

Further megatrends such as *globalization or social responsibility* are concerned with increasing effects of a globalized economy and the growing demands towards intercultural management and cooperation. Corporate social responsibility, as well as ecological responsibility, is increasingly demanded, even beyond enterprise boundaries. Leaders should be aware of the consequences of their actions. Even if working conditions at the supplier end are unacceptable, the responsibility will increasingly be traced to management and corporate level. Society no longer accepts companies' refusal of responsibility or their lack of proactive engagement.

Management of diversity means to encourage cultural diversity, to support activities in different countries, to think globally and be open to new experiences. Sustainable management will accept responsibility for social and environmental consequences of management decisions. Diversity leadership will involve monitoring the impact of actions in the company, to encourage transparency and to bring this change-process in thought and action.

Top-down always is the only way you can begin a cultural change. (Edgar Schein)

Leadership means shaping the future and for this we use the approaches, experiences and models that are known to us today. Is this approach sufficient or are we facing something new? Leadership is diverse, takes place under a variety of conditions and is substantially shaped by how leaders cope with this task as a person while maintaining relationships with others. In society and the economic order, major upheavals and changes are taking place. These changes have a huge influence on the working environment in organizations and consequently on leadership requirements and challenges.

The most important and exciting leadership task of the future will be to connect different people and their diverse skills, expectations, resources, motivations, national origins, talents, sexes and ages together! To lead diversity requires an individual leadership style in many ways. A sensitive approach, consisting of fearless leadership, punishment but with empathy and clear instructions will help to deal with different needs and skills.

To establish attractive working and leadership contexts for employees, it is necessary to contemplate the success factors in the future of leadership. Organizations must confront their values and ask: "What do we stand for today and in the future?" Which developments and changes are necessary, feasible and compatible with current and future needs? Leaders are in demand who care for the organization, the organizational culture, the employees and for themselves. Every organization and every company will need to deal with their own specific challenges of the future. Responding quickly, and flexibly, to change is particularly important for large organizations. Small and medium enterprises are inherently more flexible, but possess fewer resources to monitor multiple changes and to invest in the future. An important future challenge will be to analyze the multiple demands that lie ahead, and to assess their significance for the company. With a clear vision and a proactive alignment of the strategy, a corresponding evaluation of strategy and action, and future-oriented human resource management, the right conditions are set to create an adaptable organization.

Social processes in organizations are subject to certain interaction dynamics and will be influenced by these dynamics in the future. Networking principles, personal relationships, how people deal with undefined leeway in organizations, trust and social proximity to people who are similar to us (and less with people who are different to us, even though diversity is considered enriching) etc. trigger organizational dynamics, which will develop similarly in new working environments (see Pfeffer, 2013). And yet the leaders of tomorrow are expected to satisfy all the growing demands of individualization, of a diversified workforce with regard to age, gender and cultural background and new forms of communication in a globally connected world.

For these growing demands on leaders, the necessary skills are identified by the interviewees. The proposed "new leaders" will need extensive cognitive and emotional capacities and competencies. They hold expertise in organizational dynamics, effective interactions and communication. They will speak different languages, have a wide repertoire of hard and soft skills (including statistical, interpersonal, and questioning) and bring heterogeneity to teams to success. In addition leaders are expected to act authentically to ensure acceptance of their actions and the successful execution of challenging tasks.

In order for leaders to cope with increasing levels of diversity, while faced with increasing pressure on performance and time, resilience is strongly in demand. Leaders walk the line between "burning" for a task, without "burning out". In this, leaders must find their own way. This will involve reflecting on the leadership situation and their own experience and behavior, by creating positive contacts and exchange, appreciating themselves and others and making time for compensation, leisure and wellbeing.

3.4 Anything New or Same Old Same Old?

When discussing these topics with the experts, and later with various different practitioners, it was difficult to distinguish between "today" and "tomorrow". Leaders are already facing a number of challenges. The speed, the complexity and tension of different demands will increase, on both leader and follower levels.

Many changes can't be prepared for in advance; they must be dealt with in "real time". The pressure on daily business is constant or even increases. Challenges occurring on various levels can affect the development of organizational structures and processes. Developing new ways of leading and communicating is an ongoing process and requires leaders to operate on organizational and structural levels while also interacting with a diverse range of workers. Those ideas are nothing new. However, we are facing new technological developments and a tremendous demographic change. These new work spaces and means of communicating have an impact on established processes of taking influence and arriving at decisions, which in turn require more flexible ways of acting as well as technological know-how from employees and leaders. Technological developments enable innovative forms of communication and quicker data access. In the next years, the number of older workers in industrialized nations will increase. In industrial countries, we do not only have to deal with inter-generational co-working and knowledge transfer, but we have to attract to a very rare source of upcoming new generations of locals in this changing environment. This "new" generation has – as all "new generations" before - a different self-image, and different ways of interacting and co-working at work (i.e. Bruch, Kunze & Böhm, 2010). The future of leadership is closely linked to the future of work. Employees' and leaders' expectations regarding skills, flexibility and cooperation will grow. It is about being attractive for employees who would like to engage in and shape such a development. In this respect the Millennials as the current youngest generation have more freedom in how and where they work than past generations (Riederle, 2013).

3.5 Something to Think About: Possible Action Points and Competencies

3.5.1 *Individualization*

Individualization is based on a value set with a more individual focus. To build more awareness of these values, HR managers focus on leadership development (including focus on values), code of conducts, active discussion and reflection of the values of the organization and diversity management (see German Association for People Management, DGFP, 2013)

Individualization entails that employees' motivation level for the organization decrease in the long term and individual expectations and demands will increase. How can leaders deal with this challenge?

Schein (2013) highlights the importance of good questioning skills for retrieving relevant information from employees. Effective leadership of the future considers the dependency of the leader on the follower and endorses an open and motivating communication from "bottom" to "top". The goal is to create a climate for the "humble inquirer" to pose the right questions, thereby enabling the leader to retrieve and process essential information.

Also Bradford and Robin (2004) also emphasize interaction, communication and providing accurate feedback: *"Excellence can't be demanded – so while leaders must lead by example and set high standards, they can't expect excellence by "ordering" it. If they want members to take initiative, make full use of their abilities, and perform "above and beyond"* (p. 1)

Kahwajy (2012) emphasizes the interaction between people when she states *"there is some magic in that inner space between people"* while Chaffin (2012) expects a whole generation of Millennials will demand coaching and mentoring and also sees communication and international skills as essential in the future.

Sablynski (2014) focuses on employees by highlighting that "job embeddedness", i.e. being socially integrated at work, represents one essential tool for increasing employee engagement. Job loyalty combines affective and non-affective reasons for staying with one's organization and could be one of the challenges for future leaders.

3.5.2 Transition to Flexibility

The transition to flexible modes of working and technological developments especially in the field of social media and digitalization requires technical know-how, the adaptation of learning processes and openness to change. Leaders can actively shape this process as part of the organizational culture, for instance through primary change mechanisms. Examples of these are: guiding through critical situations, acting as a role model, allocating resources or secondary change mechanisms like shaping organizational structures, systems or processes such as costumes, rituals or stories about people (see Schein, 1992).

Technological developments enable new innovative forms of collaboration such as home working, flexible working agreements, and common projects both inside and outside the organization. In the future, leaders and HRM must establish these new communication technologies and secure their implementation. Social media can be used to deal with HR issues in new and innovative ways. The German Association for People Management (DGFP, 2013) predicts change in the future work of HR management such as an increase in the use of social media for recruiting, employer branding, in further education programs and for mobile devices in personnel administration. However, guidelines must be in place for the collaborative use of social media both inside and outside of organizations together with leadership skills to lead virtual teams. Kaiser and Kraus (2014) argue that the use of big data in HR management is still in its infancy and in the future if will influence the development of decision and leadership behavior. Leaders will increasingly rely on complex data analysis tools instead of trusting their intuition and experience. Galbraith (2014) even predicts a "shift in power from experienced and judgmental decision makers to digital decision makers". Kaiser and Kraus (2014) report from Google that "all people decisions at Google are based on data or analytics" (p. 380) or developments of game apps for identifying constructs such as creativity, social intelligence or learning by mistake. Royal Dutch Shell uses its own historic data for innovative success in combination with toy data to predict the innovative success of their employees (Peck, 2013). All these developments have an impact on the future of leadership and are accompanied by critical questions related to their actual implementation. The future of leadership increasingly needs to consider additional issues of data protection regulation, ethical questions in relation to the "transparent employee" despite, or even because of, the accessibility of various data. In order to bridge this gap between data driven decisions and personal needs, leaders need to find new ways of building personal loyalty. With an increasing dissolution of solid working relations we will also witness a maceration of traditional bonds of loyalty between leader and follower (see Hay Group, 2011).

Transition to Flexibility demands a balance between internal and external processes: Eck (2014) suggests leadership to promote both "bonding" (emphasizing intra-organizational bonds built on trust, authenticity, promotion of knowledge, circular communication etc.) and "bridging" (establishing inter-organizational open networks and resources which incorporate external influences) to create balanced leadership.

3.5.3 Demography

Leaders are encouraged to develop and implement measures in collaboration with HRM, which can help to efficiently master challenges associated with the generational change, to increase women's labor force participation and women's participation rate at top management level.

A range of possible courses of actions exist and include the provision of resources for health management or ensuring a balance between phases of high work demands and phases of recovery for employees. Lifelong learning creates the necessary prerequisites for maintaining work ability of all employees, especially of older employees. In this respect, a particular focus should be put on learning how to handle new media. Leading cross generational teams values the strengths of all generations and strives to seize their benefits. A number of tools are available: Reaching from interventions for the younger and older generations to ensuring intergenerational contact. Intergenerational knowledge and value transfer can be enabled through mixed-aged working teams, cross-generational mentoring and coaching (see Eberhardt, 2015). Leaders need to be aware of how work related behavior can be differently interpreted by the different age cohorts. "We are looking for feedback to reduce our uncertainty." In comparison, the Baby-boomers are trained to get feedback if they misbehave or perform badly.

To lead gender diversity and promote female senior roles and leadership positions, leaders need to develop awareness of the differences in gender-related communication and be aware about their own gender-specific behavior (e.g. Brettschneider, 2008). Quite often social characteristics will be attributed based on group membership and will lead to respective behaviors, quite often on implicit levels (Powell, Butterfield & Parent, 2002). It is important to acknowledge these attribution processes (reframing) and to actively engage in new ways of conduct. Flexible working conditions (i.e. homework, part-time jobs) which don't damage career prospects and aspirations are necessary to create a work environment which values work-life balance, especially for working mothers and fathers. In order to create more gender-neutral ways of communication it is important to integrate women in management teams to establish different ways of interaction patterns and a dialog-oriented organizational culture. Stuber (2012) suggests introducing quotas as one tool to integrate women into leadership position. However, this approach has been widely debated in practice.

In sum, it can be stated that a diverse work force also holds diverse expectancies towards future leaders, which due to their heterogeneity, will be impossible to be met. It will be essential for leaders to understand their employee's expectancies and their personal theories about appropriate and effective leader-follower relations.

3.5.4 Rapid Social and Economic Changes

Globalization 2.0 has a substantial impact on leadership. Leaders will increasingly need cognitive and strategic thinking skills. Implementation skills alone will not be sufficient anymore. Dealing with diversity will be an additional essential skill. Management responsibilities will be shared and responsibilities need to be defined at early stages of project planning. Future leaders will need to acquire, and use, "new" skills and competencies such as multilingualism, flexibility, international mobility and the capability to lead diverse teams which do not report directly. To master this challenge new leadership forms need to be implemented, such as building personal loyalty (vgl. Hay Group, 2011). Future leadership skills will also include team work skills, acting with integrity and classical themes such as health and safety.

HR related domains supporting leaders in future leadership challenges are defined by HR managers as employer branding, expatriate and inpatriate management, international recruitment, intercultural trainings, international standardization of personnel processes and diversity management (DGFP, 2013).

3.5.5 Social Responsibility and Sustainability

Scott and Esteves (2013) postulate that *"new leaders are using sustainability to help their organizations innovate and grow"* (p. 6). Different leadership perspectives on how to implement sustainability are identified as ranging from identifying individual and organizational readiness to demonstrating ways of decreasing resistance and increasing motivation to lead change in the long-run.

System boundaries between corporate social, state and individual responsibility will need to be negotiated at regular intervals. It is an essential leadership task to recognize the extended business responsibility of the organization and to find ways of honoring this responsibility and to generating benefits for the organization and for the employees. Benefits can be identified in relation to public reputation, efficiency of processes and a resource-conserving and long-term ecological investment of resources (WEF, 2003).

The leadership study by the Hay Group (2011) emphasizes future leaders' cognitive skills in dealing with competing demands, balancing the drive for economic success, social responsibility and sustainability. Leaders of the future will be advocates for change, making business decisions which take into account the ecological and social impacts in and outside of organizations.

3.6 Leadership of the Future

The postulated megatrends have an impact on both our working environment and on future leadership tasks. We will determine the future of working spaces and leader-follower relations. A future leader will increasingly need to balance proactive and reactive leadership. The economic world experiences profound changes given digital transformation and demographic challenges. The organization and we as humans remain limited in our behavioral repertoire, tending towards activating old action patterns. Pressure to perform and the speed of change will continue to increase. Translating individual perspectives, limitations and higher-ranking expectations will be even more demanding. To meet these challenges we need resilient leaders who can deal with the respective challenges and who can repeatedly solve leadership dilemmas.

"Think Tank: The Future of leadership" is an in-depth reflection on the challenges of leadership in dealing with megatrends in society and economy. Suggestions and impulses should be given to reflect on one's own leadership, to align it proactively and lead the entrusted organization and its employees to the future. Probably the most important question is, "How can these increasing leadership dilemmas be resolved?" What kind of leadership can make an ever more heterogeneous workforce fit for the future given a rapidly changing world? How is it possible to adapt to increasing individualism, to promote lifelong learning and development without sacrificing health, individual expectations and needs of employees and yourself?

This "100-million-dollar" question cannot be answered in a general manner. Whether to take influence and refrain from influencing, to give orientation and consider individual needs, to use technological advances and critically question them needs a consideration of personal skills and deficits, contemplations of what is feasible, a vision of what is possible, as well as introspections of personal motivations to take on leadership positions. And the willingness to tackle these challenges a whole working lifetime!

Appendix

List of Interview Partners

Ajay Bam
Co-Founder and CEO at Produk.me, Lecturer in Entrepreneurship and Innovation, Haas School of Business at University of California, Berkeley, Advisor at Padloc LLC

Ed Chavin
President IMPACT Group, Founder of The Uncommon Leadership Institute

Gioia Deucher
Leader of the new swissnex office in Brazil

Claus C. Eck
Former Deputy Director Institute of Applied Psychology in Zürich

Laura Erickson
Associate Director, Head of Finance and Operations at swissnex San Francisco

Sabine Erlenwein
Director Goethe-Institute San Francisco

David Eu
President, InPhenix

Dr. Jeannie Kahwajy
CEO, Effective Interactions

Frederic Mauch
Founder, BioApply

Ken Mooyman
President, Hexagon Geosystems NAFTA

Prof. Dr. Jeffrey Pfeffer
Thomas D. Dee II Professor of Organizational Behavior, Graduate School of Business, Stanford University

T.M. Ravi
Co-Founder, The Hive

Dr. Larry Robertson
Associate Dean, Leavey School of Business at Santa Clara University

Dr. Carole Robin
Director, Arbuckle Leadership Fellows Program, Graduate School of Business at Stanford University

Prof. Dr. Chris Sablynski
Associate Professor, Eberhardt School of Business at University of the Pacific

Prof. Dr. Edgar Schein
Society of Sloan Fellows Professor of Management Emeritus

Dr. Cynthia Scott
Consultant, Core Faculty, Sustainable Leadership, Presidio Graduate School

Kate Sherwood
Founder, Execution Strategy, Managing Director

Appendix

Questionnaire

"The Future of Leadership": Major topics to be addressed during the interview
Your own perspective of leadership – what is important to you?
Let's talk about future trends of leadership:

- Trend 1: Individualization
- Trend 2: Transition to Flexibility
- Trend 3: Demography
- Trend 4: Rapid Social and Economic Changes
- Trend 5: Social Responsibility and Sustainability

The future of leadership – my personal conclusion!

Professional Roles and Responsibilities

I like to gather some background information on your role, perspectives and responsibilities.
Which describes best your current role? (more than one selection is possible)

A   entrepreneur; owner
B   leader of company
C   leader of BU
D   consultant and trainer
E   lecturer, research fellow, associate professor, professor
F   Executive education provider
G   senior leadership expert, researcher
H   senior professional (i.e. IT, product development, supply chain, HRM, sales & marketing)
I   other, _____

Prior education: _____

I like to gather some background information on your role, perspectives and responsibilities.
In which domains do hold career experience? (more than one selection is possible)

A   entrepreneurship, ownership
B   leading a company (top management position)
C   leading a business unit, executive management
D   consulting and training leadership topics
E   teaching in bachelor, master and/or executive programs
F   research and development of leadership topics, tools etc.
G   working as a professional in one or more specific domains
    (_____) please fill in

Please share the following information about your background and expertise:

A How many years have you been working in your current role?
B How many years have you been in a leadership-related role across your career?
C In which industries did you hold leading positions?
_____, _____, _____, _____

D Your experience in working with leaders resp leadership topic is gained from the following industries:_____, _____, _____, _____

1. My own perspective on the topic of leadership

1.1 What are the specific leadership requirements you are confronted with in your daily working practice?

1.2 What does strengthen you in your position and what does help you to be successful?

2. Trend 1: Individualization

We have witnessed that organizational strategies and processes can be copied, however people not! The focus on people will increase and therefore the relevance to deal with individual positions and organizational needs will get more relevant.

2.1 "Personal leadership": What kind of development do you expect for the leaders' role and tasks? What will strengthen leaders in their position and what will help them to be successful in implementing "personal leadership"?

We see that organizational structures and roles evolve and overlap at an accelerated pace, changing the definition of roles in and outside. Cooperation, interaction, overlapping personal networks, competition, and connectivity will become major elements of future leadership.

2.2 "Co-leadership": What impact do you expect from this development for leaders' role and tasks? What will strengthen leaders in their position and what will help them to be successful in implementing "co-leadership"?

Appendix

3. Trend 2: Transition to Flexibility

We see that "Generation App" and the maceration of solid structures within and outside the organization generate a liquid world with a lot of weak relations ("likes"). The relevance to give orientation will increase and be part of "liquid leadership".

3.1 "Liquid leadership": What impact do you expect from this development for leaders' role and tasks? What will strengthen leaders in their position and what will help them to be successful in implementing "liquid leadership"?

We see that the availability of "big data" increases the complexity of decision making. "Cut out" of information are "new ideas" to handle complexity. "Start. Try. Fail. Restart. Retry" or "simply try" will be helpful in different leadership situations.

3.2 "Complexity leadership": How will the role and tasks of leaders change due to the availability of "big data", "technical possibilities" and the "wish to reduce complexity" to adapt decisions to reality? What will strengthen leaders in their position and will help them to successfully manage complexity?

4. Trend 3: Demography

We see that industrial countries face a drastic demographic change. In the future more co-workers will be older. Multi-generational approaches or age-related leadership will use the strength of each age and use it for the individual and organizational benefit.

4.1 "Age-related leadership": What impact do you expect from the demographic development for the role and tasks of leaders? What will strengthen leaders in their position and help them to successfully lead diversity?

We see that the discussion about female participation in top management has increased substantially in the last years. To address the gap in representation, many EU countries have been imposing or are threatening to impose quotas. A number of scientists and practitioners speak of the existence of a specific female leadership style and argue for the necessity to assign leadership tasks to women.

4.2 "Gender-related leadership": What impact do you expect for the role and tasks of leaders if women's participation rate in top management positions will continue to increase? What will strengthen leaders in their position and help them to successfully lead gender diversity?

4.3 How can females or female leaders get supported to be successful?

5. Trend 4: Rapid Social and Economic Changes

A number of worldwide countries are facing some drastic social and economic turbulences (e. g. European economic crisis, political turbulences in Libya). The crisis has left some countries in rather unstable economic and social circumstances, threatening long-lasting prosperity and democratic principles.

5.1 "Change leadership": In view of current economic, political and social unrest, which challenges do you expect for the role and tasks of leaders in the future?

The increased unification of the economic world order and recent economic difficulty facing a number of countries globally has increased job mobility and global flexibility. The social and economic impact of this development is an increasing diversity of employees in organizations and a growing interconnectivity among economies.

5.2 "Intercultural leadership": In view of the growing internationalization of organizations and diversity of employees, which challenges do you expect for the role and tasks of leaders in the future? What will strengthen leaders in their position and what will help them to be successful?

6. Trend 5: Social Responsibility and Sustainability

In industrial countries, political actors and social authorities tend to highlight more thoroughly the significance of social and economic responsibilities of companies. Corporate social responsibility, corporate governance and sustainability will thus become more relevant for leaders.

6.1 "Sustainable leadership": What impact will these ideas of corporate social responsibility, governance and sustainability have on leaders' roles and tasks? What will strengthen leaders in their position and help them to be successful in implementing "sustainable leadership"?

Current theories and research argue that entrepreneurs tend to develop their business locally and tend to aim for more sustainable ways of economic growth. In contrast, managers are argued to have a stronger focus on quantifiable gains and hold a weaker interest in incorporating their business into local structures.

6.2 „Entrepreneurial leadership vs. Managerial leadership": What differences do you see between entrepreneurs and managers in the performance of their duties now and in the future? What differences do you see between entrepreneurs and managers practicing sustainable and socially responsible forms of leadership?

7. The Future of Leadership – my personal conclusion

7.1 After reflecting about the future of leadership, my personal opinion is that the main difference from current leadership practices to future ones will be…
7.2 What kind of leaders do we need in the future?
7.3 What kind of followers do we need in the future?
7.4 To strengthen leaders in their leadership role they need…..

The IAP Institute of Applied Psychology

The IAP Institute of Applied Psychology has been the leading institute for applied psychology in Switzerland since 1923 by means of scientifically based and transfer oriented services. The IAP is part of the Zürich University of Applied Sciences. In

1948, the first soft skill leadership training program was founded in Switzerland at the IAP, the leadership seminar. Since then the IAP has become one of the most important scientific based and practical-oriented leadership training provider in Switzerland. Input and transfer sessions of relevant leadership issues, self-awareness, development of one's own personality as well as the ability to build effective leadership relationships used to be, and still are, core elements of the leadership education.

References

Avolio, B. J., & Bass, B. M. (2004). *MLQ—Multifactor Leadership Questionnaire*. Menlo Park, CA: Mind Garden.
Bass, B. M. (1985). *Leadership and performance beyond expectations*. New York: Free Press.
Bass, B. M., & Riggio, R. E. (2006). *Transformational leadership*. Mahwah, NJ: Erlbaum.
Bauman, Z. (2007). *Liquid Times. Living in an age of uncertainty*. Cambridge, UK: Polity Press.
Bird, A., Mendenhall, M., Stevens, M., & Oddou, G. (2010). Defining the content domain of intercultural competence for global leaders. *Journal of Managerial Psychology, 25*, 810–828.
Bradford, D. L., & Robin, C. (2004). *Leadership excellence and the "Soft Skills": Authenticity, influence and performance*. Working paper, Graduate School of Business, Stanford University.
Braedel-Kühner, C., Eberhardt, D., & Meyer, M. (2011). Individualisierte altersgerechte Führung – ein Konzept im Spannungsfeld von Individualisierung und Gleichberechtigung. *Diversitas, 01*, 63–72.
Brettschneider, J. (2008). *Frauen in Führungspositionen: Anspruch und Wirklichkeit von Chancengleichheit: Eine empirische Untersuchung in Hamburger Unternehmen im Kontext der Organisationskultur*. Hamburg, Germany: Verlag Dr. Kovač.
Bruch, H., Kunze, F., & Böhm, S. A. (2010). *Generationen erfolgreich führen : Konzepte und Praxiserfahrungen zum Management des demographischen Wandels*. Wiesbaden, Germany: Gabler.
Chaffin, E. (2012). *UnCommon leadership – Investing in the millennial generation*. Retrieved from http://ezinearticles.com/?UnCommon-Leadership---Investing-in-the-Millennial-Generation&id=7157760
Classen, M. (2008). *Change Management aktiv gestalten. Personalmanager als Architekten des Wandels*. Köln, Germany: Luchterhand.
Cook, A., & Glass, C. (2014). Women and top leadership positions. Towards an institutional analysis. *Gender, Work and Organization, 21*, 91–103.
Deutsche Gesellschaft für Personalführung E.V. (Hrsg.). (2013). *DGFP-Studie: Megatrends und HR Trends 2013*. Praxispapier 3/2013.
Döring-Seipel, E., & Lantermann, E. D. (2012). Komplexität – eine Herausforderung für Unternehmen und Führungskräfte. In S. Grote (Ed.), *Die Zukunft der Führung* (pp. 153–171). Berlin, Germany: Springer.
Eagly, A. H., & Carli, L. L. (2007). *Through the labyrinth: The truth about how women become leaders*. Boston: Harvard Business School Press.
Eagly, A. H., & Chin, J. L. (2010). Diversity and leadership in a changing world. *American Psychologist, 65*, 216–224.

Eagly, A. H., Johannesen-Schmidt, M. C., & van Engen, M. L. (2003). Transformational, transactional, and laissez-faire leadership styles: A meta-analysis comparing women and men. *Psychological Bulletin, 129*, 569–591.

Eagly, A. H., & Karau, S. J. (2002). Role congruity theory of prejudice toward female leaders. *Psychological Review, 109*, 573–598.

Eberhardt, D. (2010). Strategisches Human Resource Management. In B. Werkmann Karcher & J. Rietiker (Eds.), *Angewandte Psychologie für das Human Resource Management. Konzepte und Instrumente für ein wirkungsvolles Personalmanagement* (pp. 59–86). Berlin, Germany: Springer.

Eberhardt, D. (2012). "Like it – lead it – change it" – die Führung im Veränderungsprozess. In D. Eberhardt (Ed.), *Like it – lead it – change it! Führung im Veränderungsprozess* (pp. 5–16). Heidelberg, Germany: Springer.

Eberhardt, D. (2013a, November). Teamwork der Generationen. *Personal SCHWEIZ*, 18–19.

Eberhardt, D. (2013b, September). Erfahrung im Job. *Punktum*, 6–7.

Eberhardt, D. (2013c). Die praktische Nutzung theoretischer Erkenntnisse am Beispiel der Modellentwicklung "Soziale Nachhaltigkeit im HRM". In H. Hossfeld & R. Ortlieb (Eds.), *Macht und Employment Relations* (S. 271–276). München, Mering, Germany: Rainer Hampp.

Eberhardt, D. (2015). *Generationen zusammen führen*. Freiburg, Germany: Haufe.

Eberhardt, D., Braedel-Kühner, C., & Rauch, J. (2013). Fundiertes Wissen und viel Berufserfahrung. Generation 50 plus. *Persorama*, 20–21.

Eberhardt, D., & Meyer, M. (2011). *Mit Führung den demographischen Wandel gestalten: Individualisierte altersgerechte Führung: Wie denken und handeln Führungspersonen?* Mering, Germany: Rainer Hampp.

Eck, C. D. (2014). Management-Entwicklung (ME) als strategischer Prozess. In C. D. Eck, J. Leidenfrost, A. Küttner, & K. Götz (Eds.), *Führungskräfteentwicklung*. Berlin, Germany: Springer.

Elbe, M. (2012). Management von Ungewissheit: Zukünftige Zumutungen an die Führung. In S. Grote (Ed.), *Zukunft der Führung* (pp. 173–189). Berlin, Germany: Springer.

Elkington, J. (1998). *Cannibals with forks: The triple bottom line of 21st century business*. Gabriola Island, BC: New Society Publishers.

Enste, D., Eyerund, T. & Knelsen, I. (2013). *Führung im Wandel*. München: Roman-Herzog-Institut.

Eurostat. (2013). *Beschäftigungsquote älterer Arbeitnehmer*. Retrieved from http://epp.eurostat.ec.europa.eu/tgm/table.do?tab=table&plugin=0&language=de&pcode=tsdde100

Everitt, B. (1996). *Making sense of statistics in psychology: A second-level course*. Oxford, UK: Oxford University Press.

Feld, T., Jost, W., & Scheer, A.-W. (2014). Die nächste Generation von Unternehmensanwendungen – Entwicklung des Phänomens Big Data. *Zeitschrift für Führung und Organisation, 6*, 364–371.

Galbraith, J. R. (2014). Organization design challenges resulting from big data. *Journal of Organization Design, 3*, 2–13.

Gigerenzer, G. (2008). *Bauchentscheidungen. Die Intelligenz des Unbewussten und die Macht der Intuition* (6th ed.). München, Germany: Wilhelm Goldmann Verlag.

Gottschall, K., & Voß, G. G. (Eds.). (2005). *Entgrenzung von Arbeit und Leben. Zum Wandel der Beziehung von Erwerbstätigkeit und Privatsphäre im Alltag* (2nd ed.). München, Germany: R. Hampp Verlag.

Gürtler, D. (2013). *Die Zukunft der Führung: Eine Trendstudie*. Zürich, Switzerland: Sonderegger Druck: SIB Schweizerisches Institut für Betriebsökonomie, Dokumentation.

Hay Group. (2011). *Führungskräfte für eine neue Welt: Was die Zukunft von Führungskräften verlangt* (Whitepaper). Frankfurt, Germany.

Hofstede, G. (1980). *Culture's consequences*. Newbury Park, CA: Sage.

Horx, M., Huber, J., Steinle, A., & Wenzel, E. (2009). *Zukunft machen: Wie Sie von Trends zu Business-Innovationen kommen. Ein Praxis-Guide*. Frankfurt, Germany: Campus Verlag.

House, R. J., Dorfman, P. W., Javidan, M., Dorfman, P. W., & Gupta, V. (2004). *Culture, leadership, and organizations: The Globe study of 62 societies*. London: Sage.

References

House, R. J., Dorfman, P. W., Javidan, M., Hanges, P. J., & Sully de Luque, M. F. (2014). *Strategic leadership across cultures: The GLOBE study of CEO leadership behavior and effectiveness in 24 countries*. Los Angelos: Sage.

Ilmarinen, J., & Tempel, J. (2002). *Arbeitsfähigkeit 2010: Was können wir tun, damit Sie gesund bleiben?* Hamburg, Germany: VSA.

Kahwajy, J. (2012). Dr. Jeannie Kahwajy interview. Retrieved from https://www.youtube.com/watch?v=wgUOswm-TBE

Kaiser, S., & Kraus, H. (2014). Big Data im Personalmanagement – Erste Anwendungen und ein Blick in die Zukunft. *Zeitschrift Führung und Organisation, 6*, 379–385.

Kearney, E., & Gebert, D. (2009). Managing diversity and enhancing team outcomes: The promise of transformational leadership. *Journal of Applied Psychology, 94*, 77–89.

Kotler, P., Keller, K., & Bliemel, F. (2007). *Marketing management* (12. aktualisierte Aufl.). München, Germany: Pearson Studium.

Marxer, M. (2010). Generation App. *GDI Impuls, 2*, 16–19.

Mayring, P. (2010). *Qualitative Inhaltsanalyse: Grundlagen und Techniken* (11. aktualisierte und überarbeitete Aufl.). Basel, Switzerland: Beltz.

McKinsey & Company (Ed.). (2012). *Women matter. Making the breakthrough*. New York: Author.

Muchiri, M. K., & Ayoko, O. (2013). Linking demographic diversity to organizational outcomes. The moderating role of transformational leadership. *Leadership & Organization Development Journal, 34*, 384–406.

Peck, D. (2013). *They're watching you at work*. The Atlantic, Retrieved from http://tinyurl.com/oekcqdn

Petrie, N. (2011). *Future trends in leadership development*. Center for Creative Leadership white paper.

Pfeffer, J. (2013). You're still the same: Why theories of power hold over time and across contexts. *The Academy of Management Perspectives, 27*, 269–280.

Piscione, D. P. (2013). *Secrets of Silicon Valley*. New York: Palgrave Macmillan.

Powell, G. N., Butterfield, D. A., & Parent, J. D. (2002). Gender and managerial stereotypes: Have the times changed? *Journal of Management, 28*, 177–193.

Reichert, D. (2012). Liquid Democracy für Unternehmen. *GDI Impuls, 2*, 90–94.

Riederle, P. (2013). *Wer wir sind und was wir wollen*: Ein Digital Native erklärt seine Generation. München: KnaureBook.

Sablysnki, C. (2014). Job embeddedness and enthusiastic stayers: Management consulting strategies for employee retention. *Academy of Management Proceedings, 1*, 15282–15288.

Schein, E. H. (1992). *Organizational culture and leadership*. San Francisco: Jossey-Bass.

Schein, E. H. (2013). *Humble Inquiry: The gentle art of asking instead of telling*. San Francisco: Berrett-Koehler Publishers.

Scott, C., & Esteves, T. (2013). *Leadership for sustainability and change*. Oxford, UK: Do Sustainability.

Seufert, S. (2010). Kurzfristige Effekte und nachhaltige Veränderungen. *io Newmanagement, 6*, 12–16.

Stuber, M. (2012). Mythos Quote – Widerstände und Wege zu mehr Frauen in Führungspositionen. *Personal Quarterly, 1*, 10–16.

Tuomi, K., Ilmarinen, J., Martikainen, R., Aalto, L., & Klockars, M. (1997). Ageing, work, lifestyle and work ability index among Finnish municipal workers in 1981–1992. *Scandinavian Journal of Work, Environment & Health, 23*(Suppl 1), 58–65.

Van Engen, M. L., & Willemsen, T. M. (2004). Sex and leadership styles: A meta-analysis of research published in the 1990s. *Psychological Reports, 94*, 3–18.

Voß, G. G. (1998). Die Entgrenzung von Arbeit und Arbeitskraft. Eine subjektorientierte Interpretation des Wandels der Arbeit. *Mitteilungen aus der Arbeitsmarkt- und Berufsforschung, 31*, 473–487.

WCED. (1987). *World Commission on Environment and Development, United Nations. Our common future*. Oxford, UK: Oxford University Press.

WEF. (2003). *Responding to the leadership challenge*. Retrieved from http://www.weforum.org/pdf/GCCI/Findings_of_CEO_survey_on_GCCI.pdf

WHO. (2014). *World Health Statistics 2014*. Retrieved from http://apps.who.int/iris/bitstream/10665/112738/1/9789240692671_eng.pdf?ua=1

Wheatley, M. (2003). When change is out of our control. In M. Effron, R. Gandossy, & M. Goldsmith (Eds.), *Human Resources in the 21 century* (pp. 187–194). Hoboken, NJ: Wiley.

Yip, J., Ernst, C., & Campbell, M. (2011). *Boundary spanning leadership: Mission critical perspectives from the executive suite*. Center for Creative Leadership: Organizational Leadership White Paper Series.

Printed in the United States
By Bookmasters